Brain Verse

Poems and Activities That Build Literacy and Neural Connectivity

Dr. Linda Karges-Bone

Written by Dr. Linda Karges-Bone
Edited by Deborah Kopka
Original Illustrations by Ken Benner
Cover and Book Design by Patti Jeffers

Printed in the United States of America

ISBN 978-0-7877-0682-1

BRIDGING
the Gaps in Education™
Lorenz Educational Press
P.O. Box 802 • Dayton, OH 45401-0802

for other LEP products visit our website
www.LorenzEducationalPress.com

DEDICATION

This book is for Carolyn Marie, Audrey Jayne, and Mary Katherine,
My Precious Baby Girls

AUTHOR'S MESSAGE

The purpose of *Brain Verse: Poems and Activities That Build Literacy and Neural Connectivity* is to offer teachers and parents a language-rich, sensory-driven set of experiences through which they can teach basic academic skills. A collection of 12 rhyming story-poems has been designed to be read aloud to young children and followed with activities and lessons designed to build neural connections, especially those ties to the five components of literacy: phonics, phonemic awareness, fluency, vocabulary, and text comprehension.

Table of Contents

Dear Teachers and Parents,

When working with the brains of young children, professionals talk of building **schema** or **background knowledge**. We need a "chunk" of information, connected concepts and ideas on which to "hook" new knowledge. This is called **neural scaffolding**. These terms and a few others appear in the glossary to help you use the poems and activities along with the embedded icons with more confidence. Here is your first "chunk" of **schema**.

Children love poetry. They are instinctively drawn to the musical sounds, the alliteration, the active nature of rhyming words.

Yet, few teachers or parents use poetry often or thoroughly. We collect marvelous children stories and books, but we neglect poetry. Perhaps we subconsciously associate poetry with unpleasant high school or college literature courses or with romantic ballads on greeting cards.

That is a mistake. Poetry is ideal for young children. Typically, poems are shorter than stories, which make them appropriate for a shorter attention span. Poetry is moving and active, just like young children. The sense of rhyme, which makes the words more fun and festive, attracts children to the *reasons* for the poem.

This book uses **rhymes to teach reasons**. From holidays to telling time, 12 early childhood themes are brought to life with a poem and matching enrichment activities. Each set features **brain-friendly icons** to help you target the learning to the emerging skill.

While you are reading the poems aloud, don't forget to enjoy them yourself. When was the last time you read a poem aloud just for the fun of it? Your enthusiasm and passion for words and ideas, and indeed all learning, are the most powerful incentive for any child.

With best wishes as you build healthy young brains,

Linda

Dr. Linda Karges-Bone
Summerville, South Carolina
March 2012

Chapter One

Background Knowledge or Schema for Teachers and Parents

The Multiple Intelligences

There are different ways to be "smart," and young minds should be encouraged to develop their unique styles and innate abilities. The Theory of Multiple Intelligences (MI), which is attributed to Dr. Howard Gardner and illustrated in the figure below, is woven throughout this book and embedded into the icons. Use the simple checklist in the table on page 6 to gain perspective on the MIs each child exhibits. Do a checklist for each child.

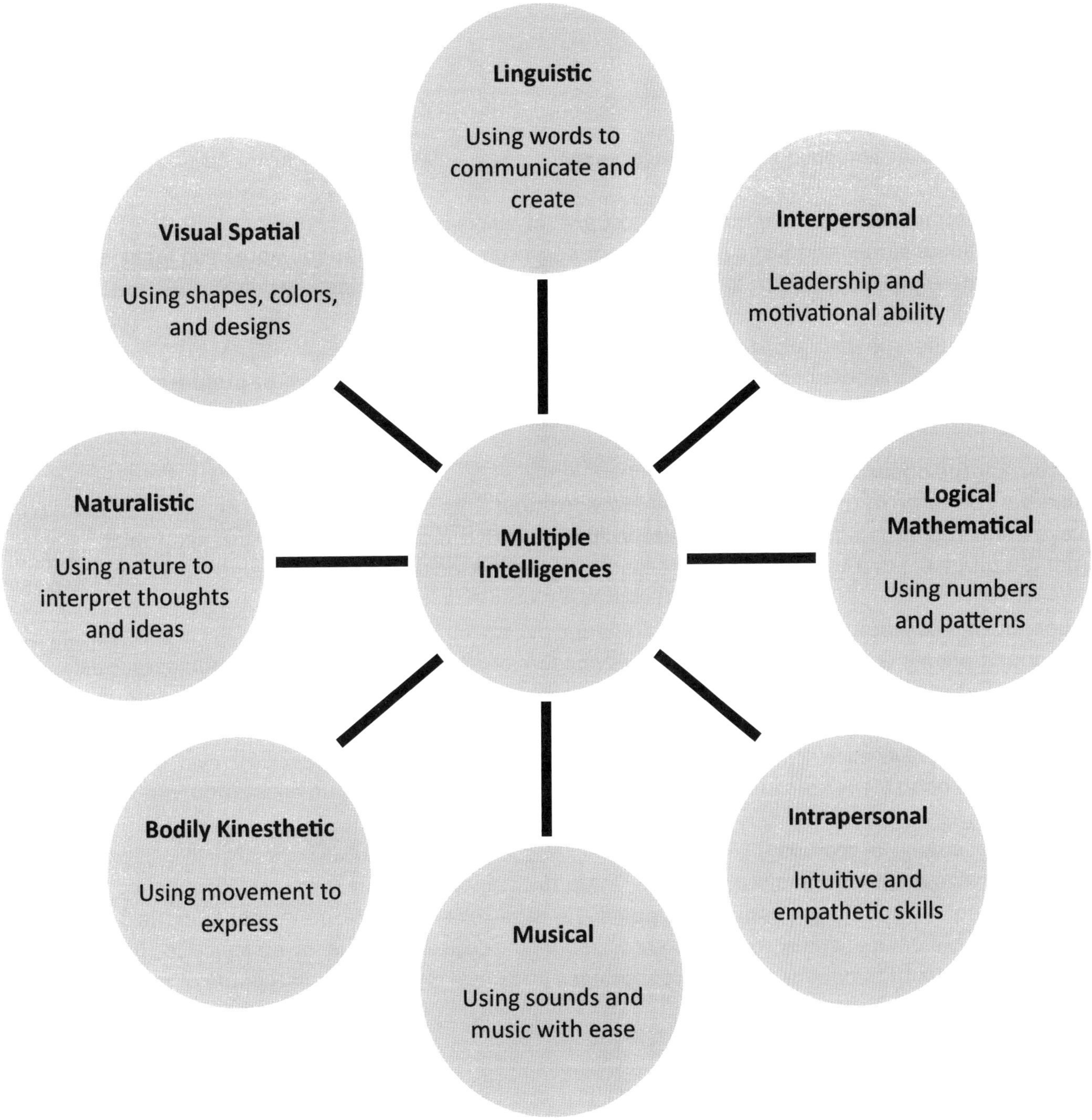

Multiple Intelligences Assessment: Different Ways to Be Smart

Circle each attribute you observe frequently in the child.

Student Name _______________________________   Date _______________________

Linguistic	Logical Mathematical	Bodily Kinesthetic	Visual Spatial	Musical	Intrapersonal	Interpersonal	Naturalistic
Speaks fluently	Counts and sorts with ease	Physically strong and sure or himself/ herself	Chooses the art center or easel often	Sings and makes up tunes without prompting	Volunteers to help do tasks or to "be first"	Shows interest in others' health and well being	Finds objects outdoors and shares them
Likes to hold and read books	Groups objects intuitively	Lots of physical energy	Shows detail in drawing or writing	Plays an instrument with skill for his or her age	Children look to him or her as a leader in games	Comforts other children	Has interest in weather and geography
Makes up stories to tell or write	Notices details like height/weight and is accurate	Accuracy in throwing, skipping, hopping, jumping	Interested in colors and textures	Moves his or her body in rhythm during daily activities	Competitive in games and learning	Creative and thoughtful in games and learning	Likes caring for animals and/or plants
Likes library time	Likes puzzles or computers	Likes physical education	Likes art class	Likes music class	Likes events that have a "winner"	Likes the guidance or religion sessions	Likes outdoor lessons or field trips
Chooses books for free time	Chooses puzzles for free time	Chooses blocks or balls for free time	Chooses crayons for free time	Chooses music or dance for free time	Chooses to talk or complete a project with others at free time	Chooses to play in house-keeping for free time	Chooses the science table or fish tank for free time
Described as "expressive"	Described as "analytical"	Described as "active"	Described as "creative"	Described as "artistic"	Described as "a leader"	Described as "sensitive"	Described as "outdoorsy"

Using This Book

Each section of *Brain Verse: Poems and Activities That Build Literacy and Neural Connectivity* features a poem and accompanying activities and lesson prompts to build language and critical thinking in young children. There are 12 kinds of activities, each associated with a **brain-building icon(s)** to assist teachers and parents in applying the skills under development. When you see each icon, consider how the activity is helping in developing a specific kind of cognitive skill with which it associated. Send this page home to parents to familiarize them with your mutual goals for brain development. Below is a list of the icons used throughout this text.

Affective Domain or
Emotional Intelligence

Auditory Discrimination,
Auditory Memory, Listening

Critical Thinking and
Schema Building

Creativity and Right Brain
Thinking

Expressive and
Receptive Language

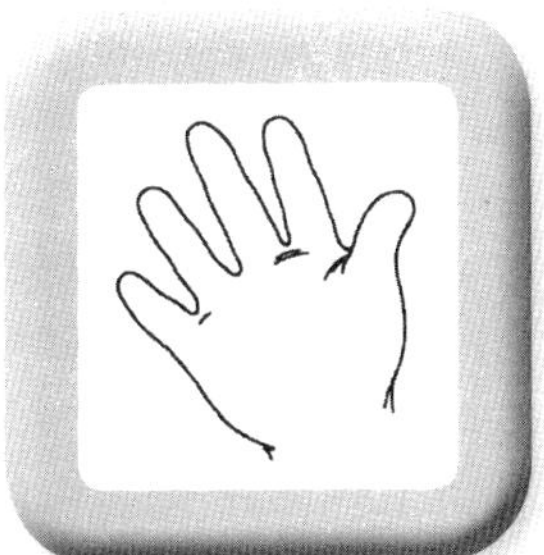

Fine Motor Development

Numerical Fluency

Organization of Thoughts
and Materials

Patterns and Sequences

Phonics and Phonemic
Awareness

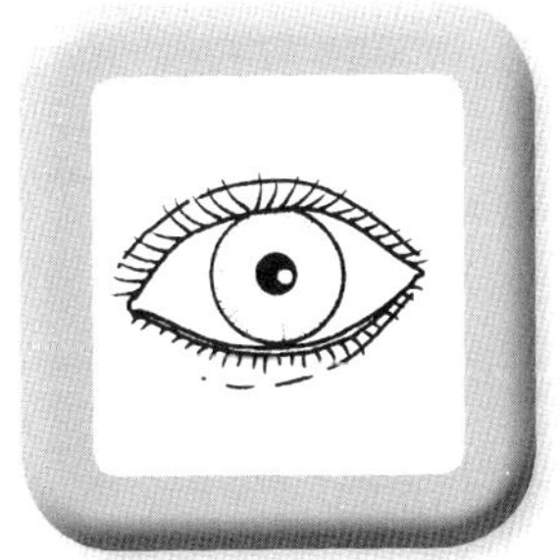

Visual Discrimination and
Visual Memory

Vocabulary and Fluency

Early Childhood Skills Checklist

Directions: Use this checklist to monitor each child's progress over the course of the year. Copy one sheet for each child, and the checklist, along with materials from these units and from other lessons, in a portfolio.

Student _________________________________   School Year______________   Teacher _________________________

Skill	Progress	Competent	Growing	Weak
Expressive language				
Receptive language				
Counting and number recognition				
Visual discrimination				
Phonics and phonemic awareness				
Fine motor development				
Gross motor development				
Critical thinking				
Listening and auditory memory				
Socio-emotional skills				

Glossary for Teaching with the Brain in Mind

amygdala: Almond-shaped structures in the front of the brain that "turn on" when a child is under stress.

auditory discrimination: The ability to detect differences between and among sounds or phonemes.

auditory memory: The ability to recall what one has heard or how sounds are unique.

Bloom's Taxonomy: A hierarchy of six levels of thinking, from simple to complex.

Broca's area: Area of the left frontal lobe associated with speech and expression of language.

cognition: The formal word for thinking.

constructivism: The philosophy of education in which children create their own schema or understanding through active engagement and participation.

cortisol: The stress hormone that can impede higher levels of thinking.

creativity: Using existing knowledge and observations in fresh ways.

critical thinking: A type of thinking in which the brain grows and stretches and makes new connections.

expressive language: The sum of words or expressions that a child can speak or use without assistance.

fine motor skill: Using the hands and fingers to develop small movements such as writing, coloring, and cutting.

fluency: The ability to use words with ease and to read with expression.

metacognition: Thinking about thinking. The kind of work teachers do as they try to get inside the brains of children to help them acquire new skills.

multiple intelligences: Dr. Howard Gardner's model of how our brain(s) work. There are eight different ways to be intelligent.

neural plasticity: The ability of a young brain to grow and change rapidly.

neural scaffolding: Bridging from one thought to another by using context clues and coaching.

neurons: Technical name for nerve cells in the brain.

numerical ability or reasoning: The skill of working with numbers and the concepts attached to numbers.

patterning: The ability to recognize and create patterns with words, shapes, and objects.

phonics: Identifying and recognizing letters and the speech sounds or *phonemes* associated with them.

phonemic awareness: The ability to recognize and use rhyming words.

pre-frontal cortex: The front of the brain or gray matter where higher-order thinking takes place.

receptive language: The sum of words and expressions that a child can understand or recognize.

schema: Chunks of concepts that go together to build ideas and understanding.

synapses: Connections between nerves; where thinking and learning grow.

text comprehension: Understanding what one has read or heard.

visual discrimination: The ability to identify and differentiate forms, patterns, shapes, and eventually letters and words.

vocabulary: The ability to recognize and use words in context.

Brain Break: A Verse to Remember

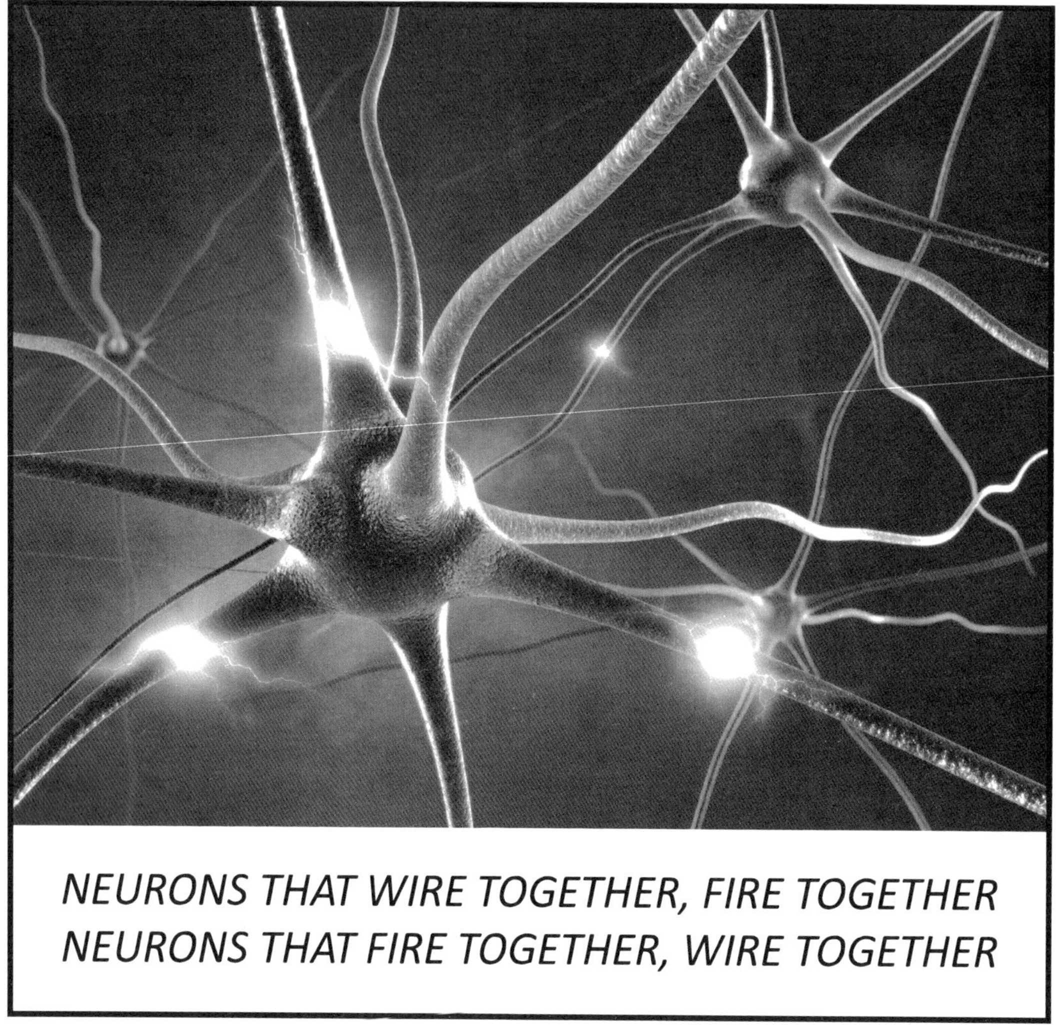

Poetry and other brain-building activities help to build a more "plastic," richly connected young brain by repeating and linking words and ideas.

Chapter Two

Keeping Promises:
Building New Ideas and Brain Cells in the New Year

Keeping Promises

"I promise to clean my room every day."
"I promise to keep my skates out of the way."
"I promise to listen to everything you say."
Promises, promises . . . which ones will stay?

"I fixed my bed, but forgot the floor."
"Oops . . . there's a roller blade left by the door."
"Sorry, I won't talk back anymore."
Promises, promises . . . easy to ignore!

"I'll clean up the mess when I get back home."
"How did that ice skate end up by the phone?"
"I'll try not to use that rude, bossy tone."
Promises, promises . . . left all alone.

"I just didn't see it, those clothes in a pile."
"Sorry, I'll park my bike in just one more mile."
"Okay, mom, I can try to answer with a smile."
Promises, promises . . . they're just not my style!

"Did you say clean . . . C-L-E-A-N?"
"Who left my red wagon in the middle of the den?"
"Ugh, oh, I talked back to you again."
Promises, promises . . . where will they end?

It is New Years and time for promises galore.
Promises to listen, to help out and more.
But who could tell what life has in store?
Do I have to keep promises? What for?

A promise is a promise, a trust that you earn.
Keep your promise close and take your turn
At trying to show grown-up concern.
With promises to help out, to listen, and learn.

Brain-Building Activities

Read "Keeping Promises" on **page 11** to children and then invite each child to respond to the question: "What is a promise?" Using chart paper and a scented green marker (to stimulate thinking), record each child's response. Be sure to read each response aloud back to the group after it is recorded.

Draw children's attention to several words in "Keeping Promises" on **page 11** that may be unfamiliar, including *bossy, galore, concern, tone, style, trust*, and *earn*. Write each word on the board, and guide children in using context clues from the poem to figure out what the words mean.

Use Reproducible 1: Color by Number, Traced Verse, and Handwriting Practice on **page 14** to develop fine motor and visual discrimination. The children can trace the verse, and then, on the bottom line, copy the verse.

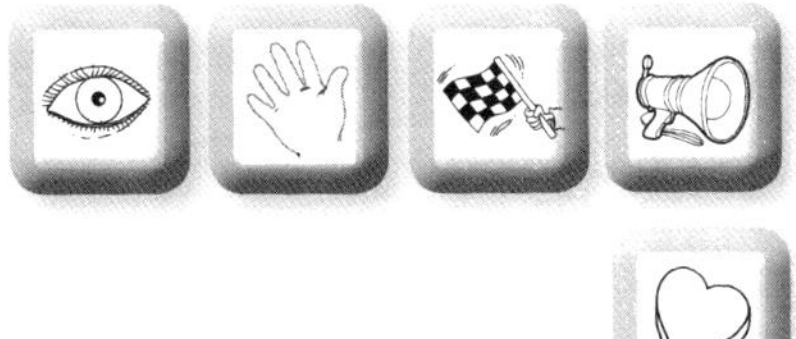

Sometimes children need to practice articulating the sounds B, D, and P. Use Reproducible 2: Listen and Learn on **page 15** to reinforce auditory and visual discrimination among the children.

Use "Keeping Promises" on **page 11** to introduce the concept of tone of voice. As the children sit in a circle around you, practice using several varied tones as you repeat a command such as, "Let's go now." Try to make your voice happy, angry, bossy, silly, light, deep, etc. Then invite the children to "Name That Tone." Switch it around and have the children create their own voice inflections and associate them with words.

Continue with "Name That Tone" by printing tone words on a large index card. Include words such as: LOUD, SOFT, SWEET, GENTLE, BOSSY, GRUMPY, MEAN, ANGRY, HURRIED, WORRIED, LIGHT, DEEP, DARK, KIND, and SILLY. Put the word cards into a basket, and let the children take turns drawing them out and playing charades with them. The first child to "Name That Tone" gets to take the next card.

Discuss how different tones of voice and expressions affect our feelings and dispositions. Ask children to share both positive and negative feelings and help them to identify and give voice to them.

Use Reproducible 3: Finding Our Way to the New Year Maze on **page 16** to practice fine motor skills.

Start the new year right by reinforcing counting skills. If you have not already done so, start a timeline for your class, beginning with the first day of school. Use adding machine tape, and run the timeline at kids' level around the room. Each day you are in school, a child records the number of the day. Go back to Day One, and practice counting by groups of 5; circle the numbers in the series with *red* marker: 10, 15, 20. Then go back and count by groups of 10; circle those numbers with a *green* marker: 10, 20, 30, 40. Ask, "Why do you think some of the numbers have *both* a red and a green circle?"

Did you know that peppermints can help children to remember? Use a bag of wrapped peppermints or spearmints to help children solve the simple equations on Reproducible 4: Peppermint Promises Math, **page 17**.

Help children to develop fine motor skills by making a "Promises, Promises" booklet. Use Reproducible 5 on **page 18**, and instruct children to write their promises on each page of the booklet. One of your small rectangles will be the cover sheet. Each child should (1) cut out his or her squares; (2) put them in numerical order; and (3) staple the finished booklet.

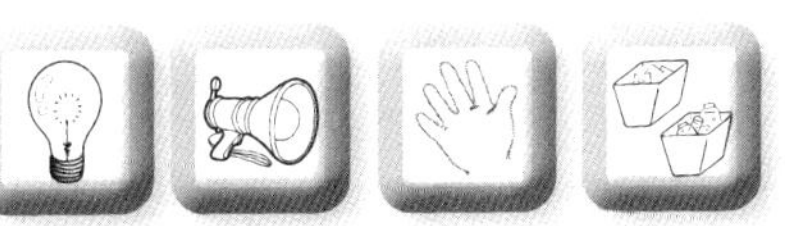

Children can use the Connect-the-Dots activity on Reproducible 6, **page 19**, to practice counting and sequencing skills.

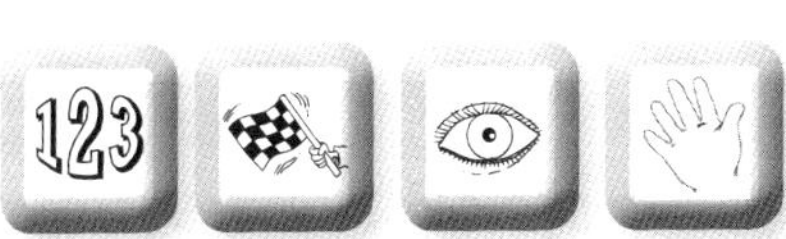

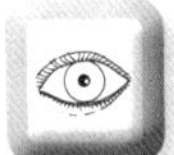    

My name is: _________________________________ .

Color by Number

Directions: Color by number this picture.

1 – brown
2 – dark blue
3 – yellow
4 – red
5 – gray
6 – peach
7 – light blue
8 – purple

Traced Verse

Directions: Trace the verse.

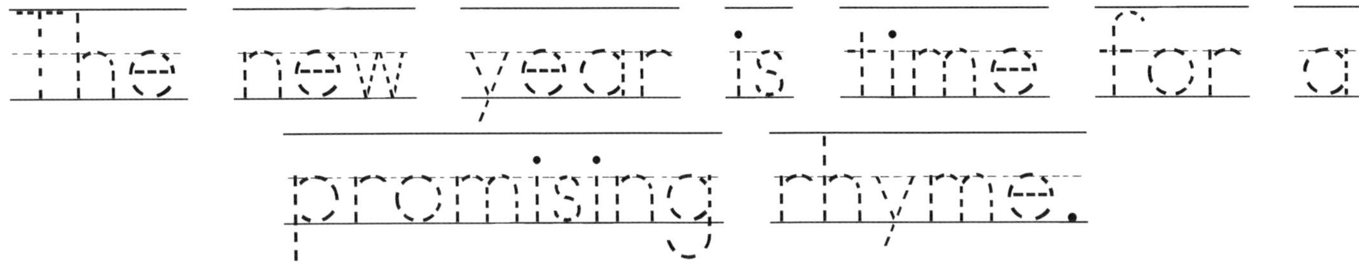

Handwriting Practice

Directions: Now copy the verse on the line below.

Reproducible 2: Listen and Learn

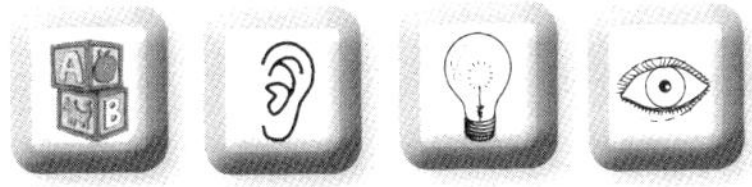

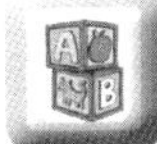

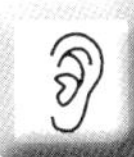

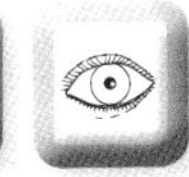

My name is:____________________________ .

Directions: Listen carefully as your teacher says the name of each item. In the line under the picture, write the letter D, B, or P to show the letter and sound that begins each word.

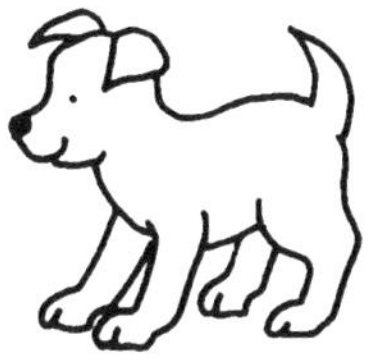

____

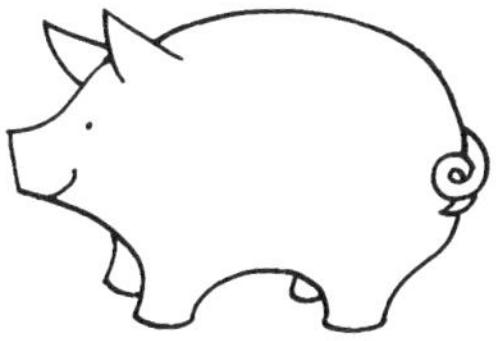

____

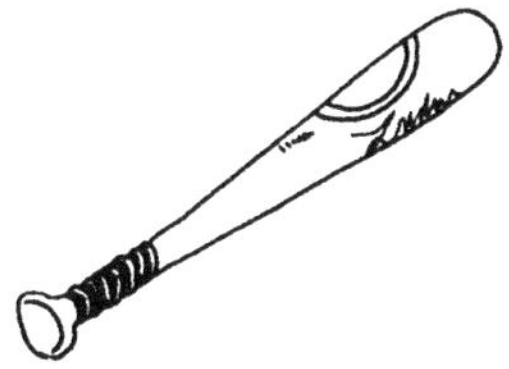

____

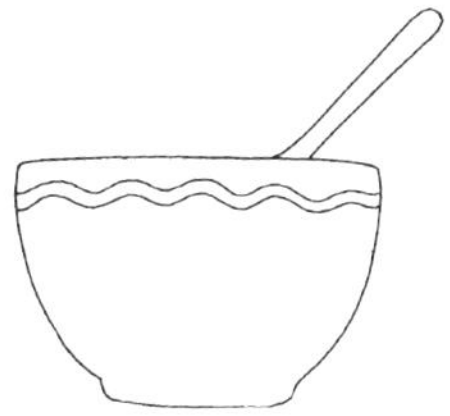

____

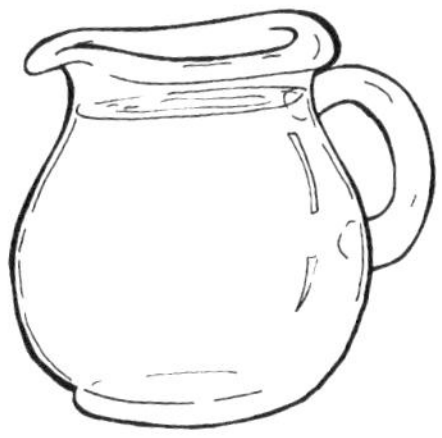

____

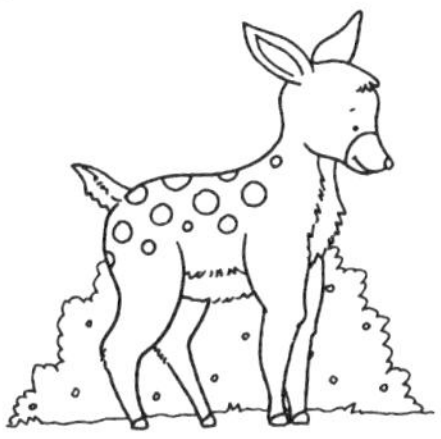

____

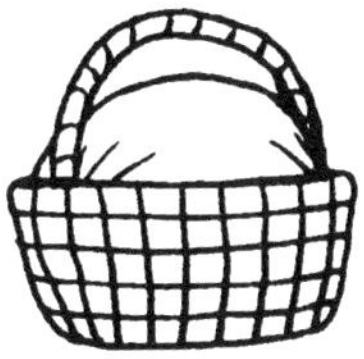

____

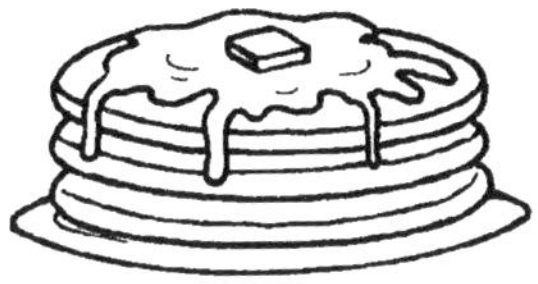

____

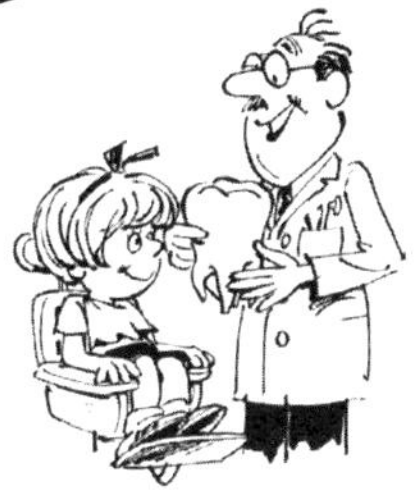

____

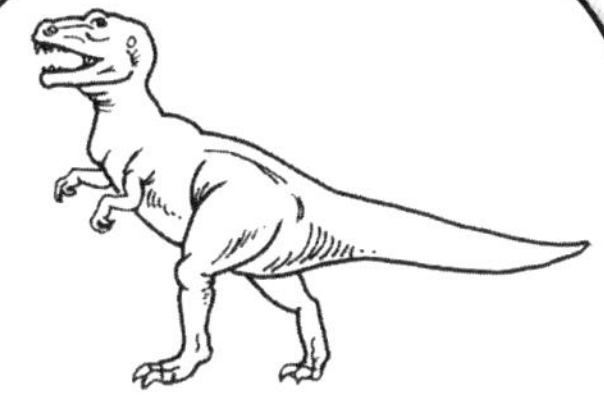

____

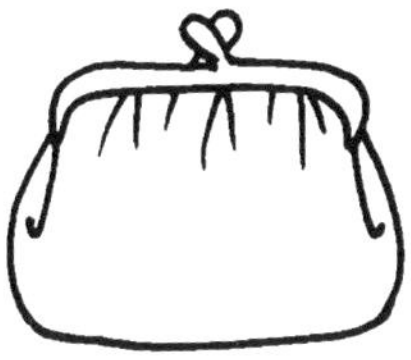

____

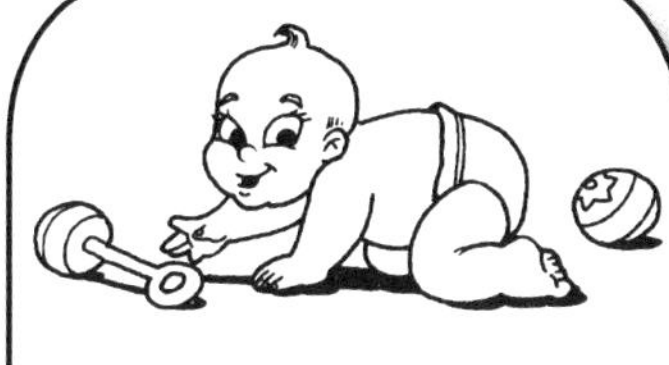

____

Reproducible 3: Finding Your Way to the New Year Maze

   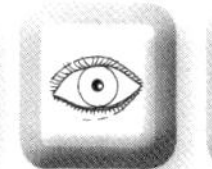

My name is:______________________________ .

Directions: Place your pencil on the dot that says "Begin," and find the shortest, clear path to the New Year's Baby. At the bottom of the page, complete the sentence by using numbers to name the old year and the new year.

Begin

The old year was ________________ .

The new year is ________________ .

My name is: _______________________________ .

Directions: You should have a small pile of wrapped peppermints to help you solve each problem. Stack the right number of mints in the box to show the answer to the problem. Write the answer on the line with your pencil.

$2 + 1 =$ _______

$3 - 1 =$ _______

$4 - 0 =$ _______

$1 + 3 =$ _______

$3 + 2 =$ _______

$2 - 2 =$ _______

My name is: _______________________________ .

Directions: Keeping promises is important. Think about five promises that you want to make and keep during this new year. Write or ask your teacher to write each promise on a page of the booklet. Cut out the pages, and place the cover page on top. Put the pages in order. Color the cover page, and then staple the booklet together.

_________'s

Promises Book for

____

1

I promise to

____

____

____

2

I promise to

____

____

____

3

I promise to

____

____

____

4

I promise to

____

____

____

5

I promise to

____

____

____

Reproducible 6: Connect the Dots

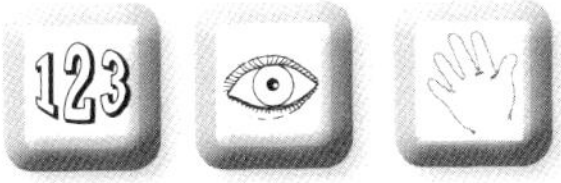

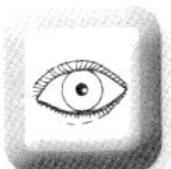

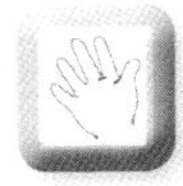

My name is: ______________________________ .

Directions: Place your pencil on the number 1 and connect the dots in order. What picture did you make?

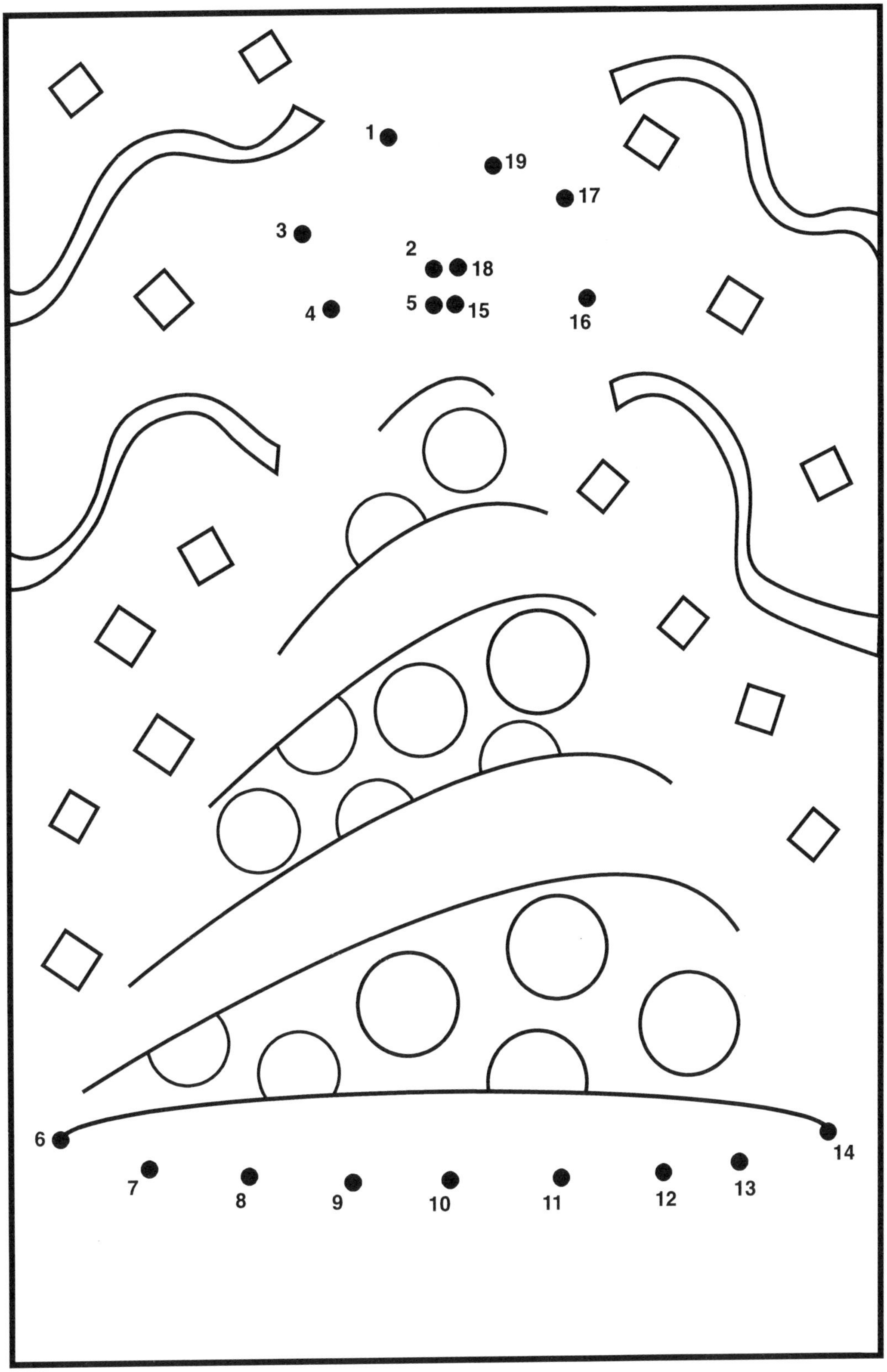

This is a picture of: ______________________________.

Chapter Three

The Biggest Valentine:
Thinking About Sizes and Valentine Surprises

The Biggest Valentine

Who has a bigger heart than mine?
Show me a greater valentine,
One with a longer curving line,
One with more glitter, sparkle, and shine.

I have a valentine that is tall,
Three feet high, halfway up the wall,
Made from tissue paper crumpled into balls,
Certainly the best valentine of all.

Look at this heart, fat and wide!
It's at least twelve inches from side to side,
Shiny with paper, paint and, pride,
And sequins and jewels, carefully applied.

Look at my heart, soft and deep,
A pillow valentine, to take to sleep,
Thick with cotton stuffed like sheep,
The biggest valentine you'll want to keep.

What about a valentine that weighs five pounds?
Filled with nuts and candies so round,
And papers that make a rustling sound
When your favorite piece of chocolate is found?

Bigger, fatter, thicker, taller,
All seem better than mine that is smaller.
But I made it for you, with loving care,
A special message written there.

So remember this when sizes win:
All that matters is the thought within.
The biggest valentine has the greatest caring,
Coming from a heart that is made for sharing.

Brain-Building Activities

After reading "The Biggest Valentine" on **page 20** aloud to the children, ask the following questions: (1) Is bigger always better? (2) Does it matter if you receive a small valentine or a large valentine? (3) What is "the thought within?" (4) How do valentines show others how we feel?

Tell the children you will list words about sizes they heard in the poem. Write the words on chart paper using a red-scented marker for emphasis. The size words include *bigger, smaller, taller, thicker, greater, longer, more, inches, feet, deep, weighs,* and *pounds.*

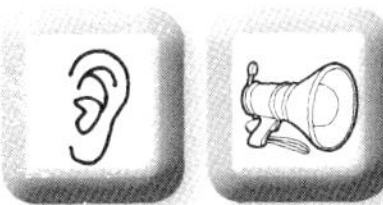

Use Reproducible 1: Color by Number, Traced Verse, and Handwriting Practice on **page 23** to develop fine motor and visual discrimination. The children can trace the verse, and then, on the bottom line, copy the verse.

Create a class book using Reproducible 2 on **page 24**. Children complete the prompt that says: "If I could make you the biggest and best valentine, it would have ________________." Encourage the use of descriptive words and longer sentences. Compile the individual pages into a class book.

Practice auditory discrimination skills with the children by doing Reproducible 3: Listen and Learn: Discrimination of Ending Consonant Sounds on **page 25**. Children are to listen as you read each word and write the letter *T* or *R* under the picture that is represented.

Give each child a large sheet of finger paint paper or sturdy art paper. Instruct each child to print the phrase *Caring and Sharing* in the center of the paper. Then, give children pink and red finger paints and heart-shaped sponges. Let them create a Valentine's Day display that frames the phrase.

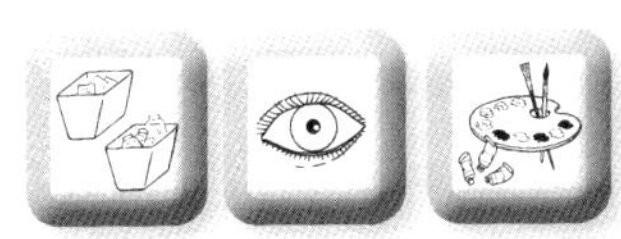

Children can use Reproducible 4: Connect the Dots on **page 26** to practice counting and sequencing skills.

To practice counting skills, give each child a small cup of confection hearts and Reproducible 5: How Many Hearts? on **page 27**.

Use cubes or blocks to practice concepts of size. Have children work in pairs or small groups. Give each group an equal number of blocks or cubes to use to solve challenges. Ask the groups to create a taller and shorter structure, a thin and a thick structure, a deep or shallow structure, or a bigger and smaller structure.

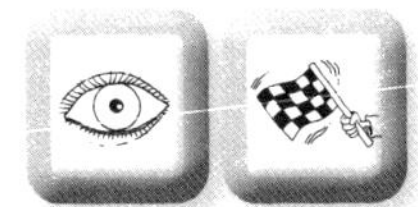

Using confection hearts once again, demonstrate how to make patterns with the candies, such as pink/pink/green or yellow/blue/yellow. After you are satisfied that the children understand the concept, give them each a cup of candies and ask them to make at least two patterns for you to come around and check.

Use Reproducible 6: Stacking Up Hearts on **page 28** to teach sequencing and observation skills. The children should cut out each of the five heart shapes and stack them with the largest on the bottom and the smallest on the top. Demonstrate to the children how to put a small dot of glue in the center of each heart to create a 3-D valentine. You may want to use white, lacy doilies as a backdrop.

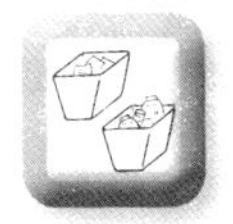

Use Reproducible 7: Sizes and Shapes on **page 29** to match shapes of different sizes. Children should cut out the cards at the bottom of the page and then paste them on top of the object that is the same shape but a different size.

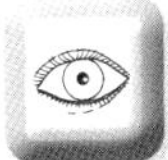

My name is: ___________________________________ .

Color by Number

Directions: Color by number this picture.

1 – red
2 – green
3 – light blue
4 – pink
5 – brown
6 – peach
7 – purple
8 – yellow

Traced Verse

Directions: Trace the verse.

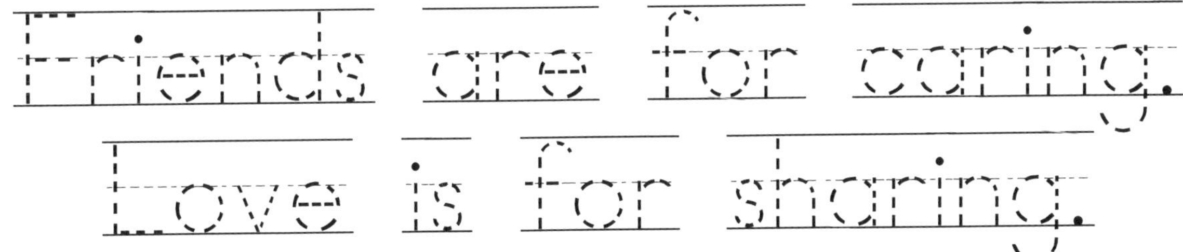

Handwriting Practice

Directions: Now copy the verse on the line below.

Directions: Complete the sentence and illustrate your page of a class book about valentines.

If I could make you the biggest and best valentine, it would have

____

____

by

My name is: ________________________________ .

Directions: Listen as your teacher reads the word for each picture.
Write the letter T or R on the line under the picture to show the sound with which the word ends.

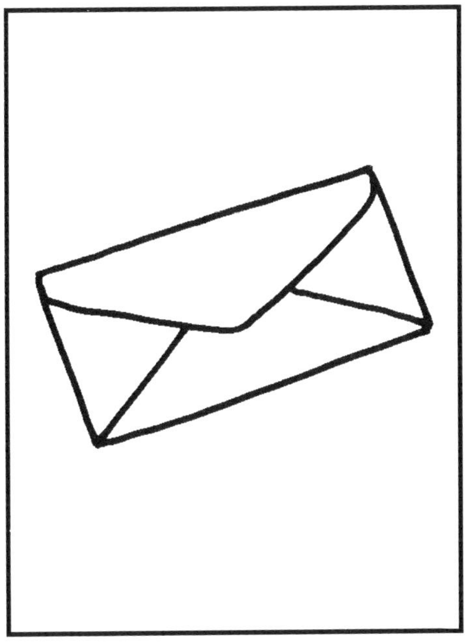

Reproducible 4: Connect the Dots

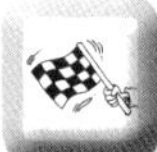

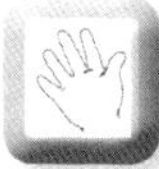

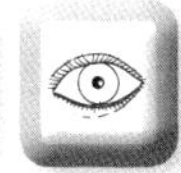

My name is: ______________________________ .

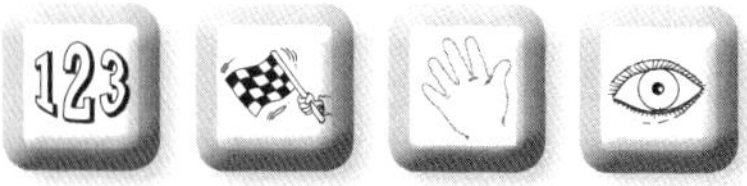

Directions: Place your pencil on the number 1 and connect the dots in order. What picture did you make?

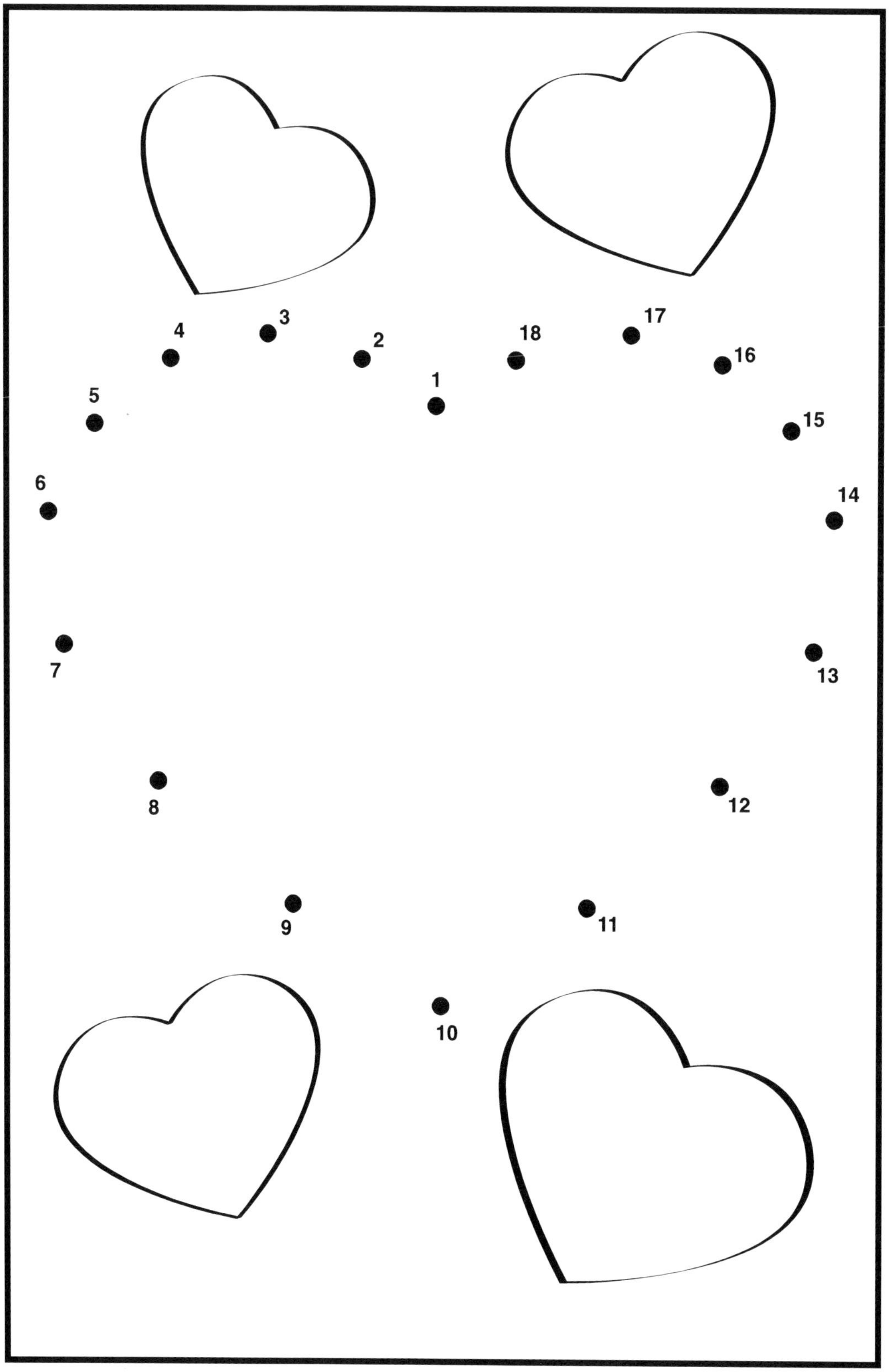

This is a picture of: ____.

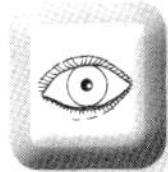 

My name is: ______________________________ .

Directions: Use your cup of candy hearts to solve the problems. You can count out the hearts to find the right answer, and then eat them! Be sure to write your answer on the line after the = sign.

Reproducible 6: Stacking Up Hearts

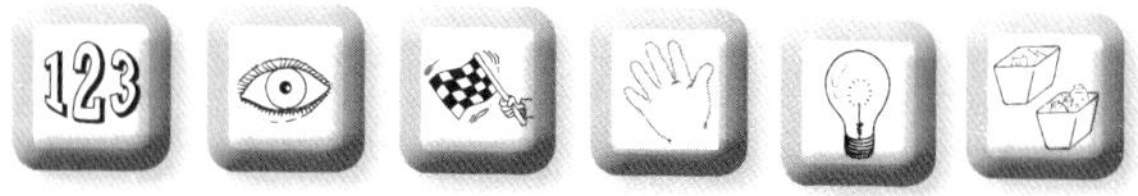

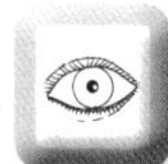

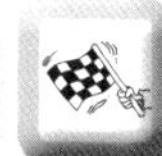

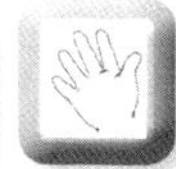

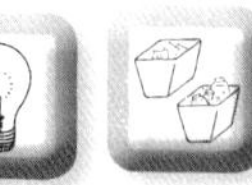

My name is: ______________________________ .

Directions: Cut out each of the five hearts on this page to make a special valentine. Stack up the hearts so the largest heart is on the bottom of the page and the smallest heart is on the top. The hearts should be in order according to size.

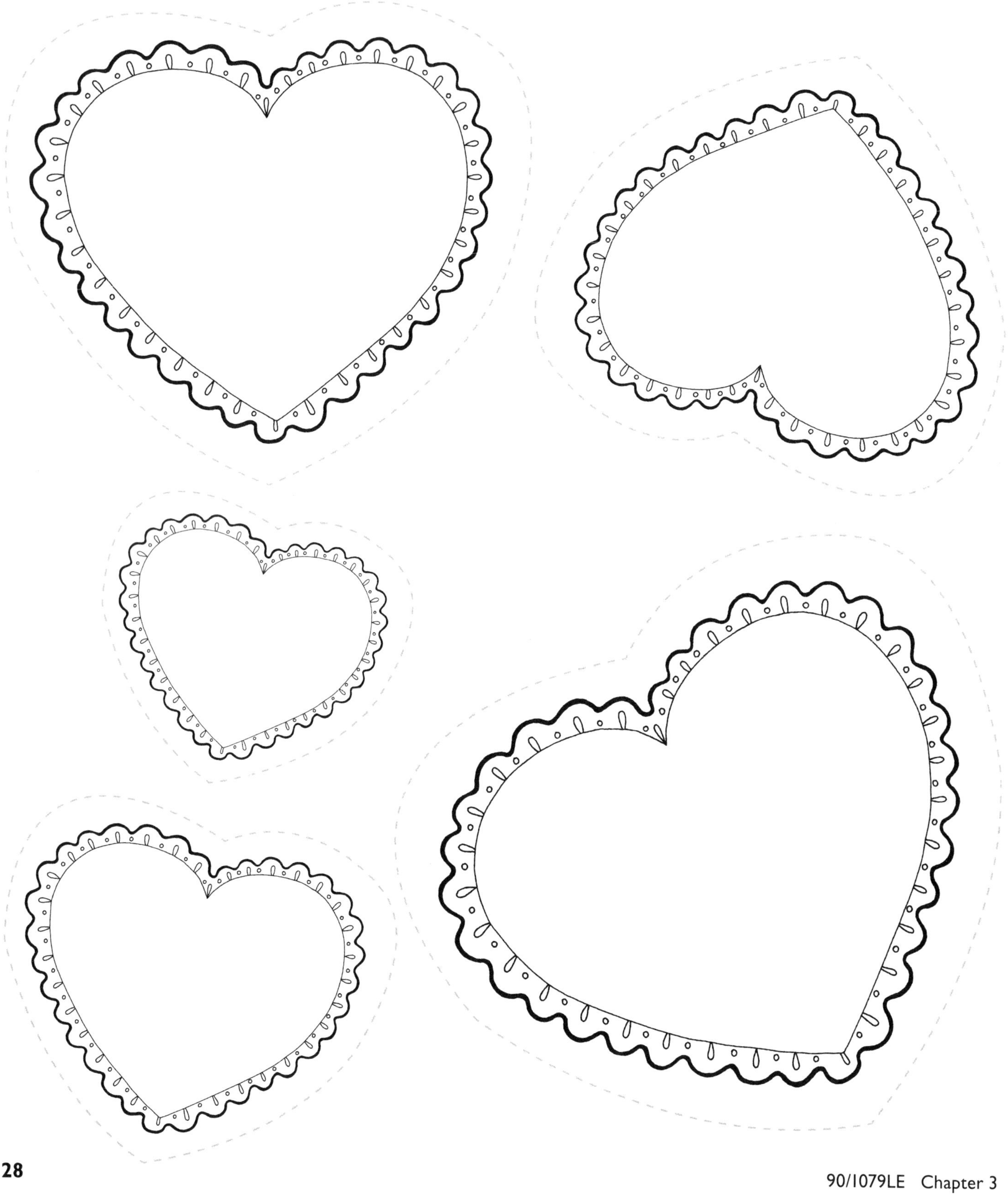

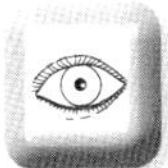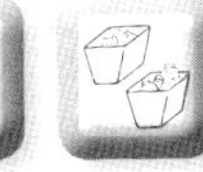

My name is: ______________________________________ .

Directions: Cut out the six shapes at the bottom of the page. Glue the shape to the larger or smaller shape that matches it. One of the sets will be *the same size*. Circle that set in red.

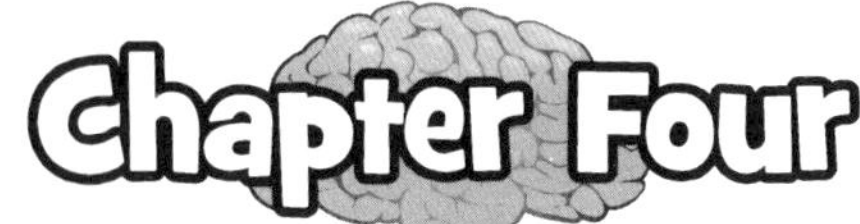

Chapter Four

Counting the Days Until Spring:
Thinking About Changing Seasons and Counting

Counting the Days Until Spring

Can you count the days til spring?
Help me with this numbering
Of colors and sounds and many things
Measuring the signs of spring.

One, two, three, four . . .
The wind is tapping at the door.
Breezy, blowing, making kites soar,
Hurry up, I'm counting more.

Five, six, seven, eight . . .
Wisteria is curling on the gate . . .
Purple blossoms can hardly wait,
Hurry up, spring can't be late.

Nine and ten, can you hear the hen?
Cackling at her chicks and then,
Scrambling away to her fresh-painted pen?
Hurry now chicks, don't be late again!

Now count backward, ten and nine.
Colors of springtime, make a line.
Purple and pink, lemon and lime,
Hurry up, summer's not far behind.

Eight and seven follow now.
The farmer is getting out his plow
For planting a garden – he knows how.
But hurry, you still must feed the cow.

Six and five, bees in their hive.
Spreading pollen, they buzz and dive.
Keeping the flowers fresh and alive,
Please hurry bees, here come the butterflies.

Four and three, a basket for me,
Filled with springtime finery.
Colored eggs and a soft bunny . . .
Hurry before he hops away from me.

Two and one, I feel the sun
Beaming warmly on everyone.
Spring is the season for growing and fun,
So hurry, before this season is done.

Brain-Building Activities

Read "Counting the Days Until Spring" on **page 30** aloud to children. Then use scented markers and a chart to record the children's responses to the following questions:

- How do we know that spring is on the way?
- How does the earth change when spring is coming?
- Can you name some other colors that appear in the spring?
- Do we wear different clothing in spring? Why?
- Why might people want spring to hurry and arrive after winter?

Use Reproducible 1: Color by Number, Traced Verse, and Handwriting Practice on **page 33** to develop fine motor and visual discrimination. The children can trace the verse, and then, on the bottom line, copy the verse.

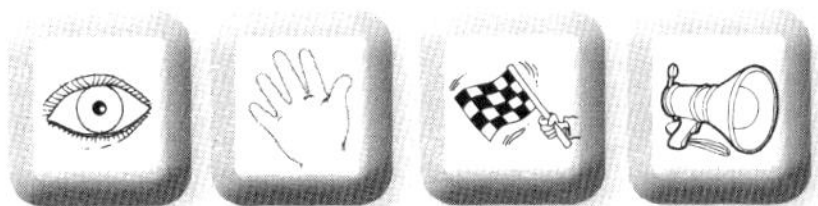

Use Reproducible 2: Spring Shapes Flip Book on **page 34** to make a book of words related to spring. Help the children to label the shapes on each page of the flip book (eggs, bird, flowers, sun, bunny, bug).

Use or make pink, purple, and yellow play clay to create eggs, spring flowers, and other spring sights. (A no-cooking-required recipe follows on Reproducible 3, **page 35.**) This page also has a sequencing and memory activity.

Have students practice fine motor and counting skills by completing Reproducible 4: Connect the Dots on **page 36**.

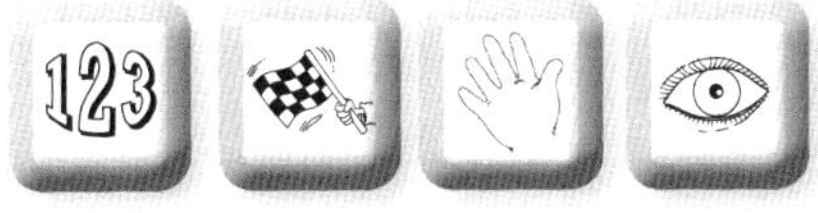

Practice counting forward and backward from 1 to 10 using Reproducibles 5 and 6: Writing Numbers on **pages 37 and 38**. Do this in a group and individually.

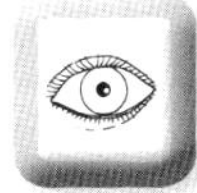

In conjunction with Reproducibles 5 and 6, use Reproducible 7: Counting Certificate on **page 39** to pass out on the first day of spring.

Invite parents to send in new or used plastic Easter eggs, the kind that pull apart so they can be "stuffed," and use them in the following ways:

- Pull them all apart and mix them up. Children can put the matching colors together and seal the eggs.

- Allow children to pull eggs apart and stuff them with wrapped candies they have sorted into groups of 2, 3, or 4.

- Use pink and yellow finger paint scented with rose or lavender oil to create "spring scenes" that can be hung around the classroom.

- Use the plastic eggs to sort into groups of 2, 3, 4, or more as you give oral directions; "Place the green eggs into groups of 2; Place the yellow eggs into groups of 3," etc.

- Use pastel-colored cupcake liners and jelly beans to tell number stories that require listening and counting. For example:

    "On the way to the market, Laura had four beans in her basket. (Children place four beans in their "baskets.") But she tripped over a tree root and dropped two beans. (Children take out two beans.) Now how many beans are in Laura's basket?"

- On the first of March, begin a countdown until the first day of spring. Place a piece of adding machine tape at "child level" and tape it to the wall. As you record each day of March on the tape, invite individual children to illustrate the day with a marker or crayons and sign it. For example, Luis might make purple flowers on March 3 and sign his name in green marker. On the first day of spring, serve a special treat.

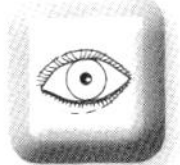    

My name is: ___________________________________ .

Color by Number

Directions: Color by number this picture.

1 – green
2 – brown
3 – blue
4 – yellow
5 – orange
6 – pink

Traced Verse

Directions: Trace the verse.

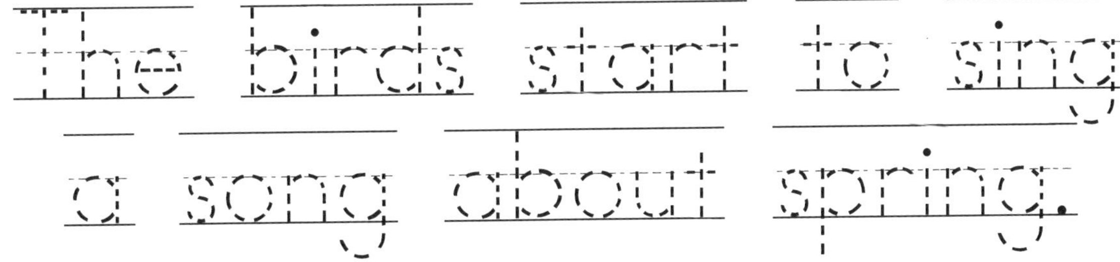

Handwriting Practice

Directions: Now copy the verse on the line below.

Reproducible 2: *Spring Shapes Flip Book*

Directions: Label and color each of the pictures below. Then cut out the pages to make your own flip book about spring!

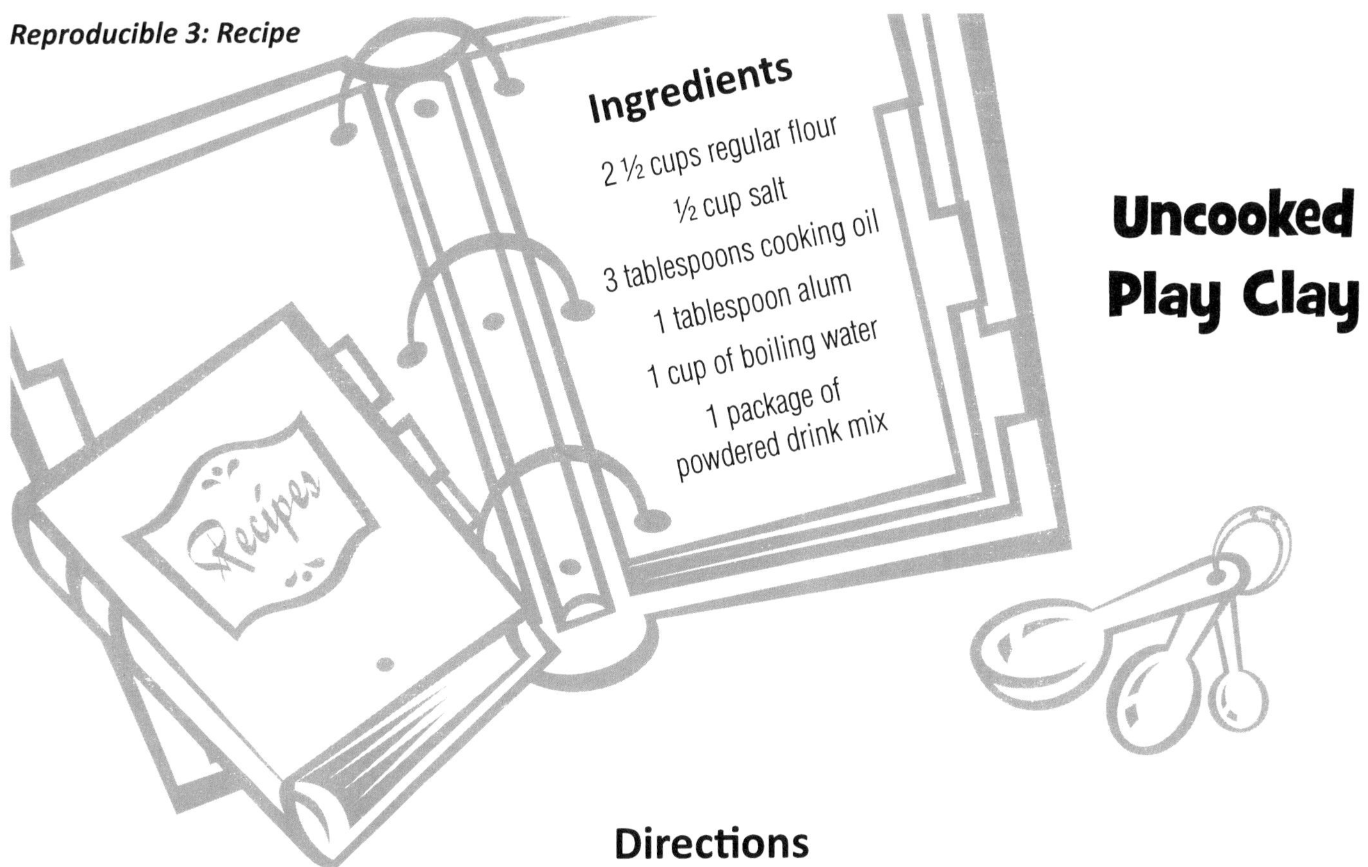

Directions

Gently mix the ingredients in a large bowl.
Add more flour or more water until the desired consistency is achieved.

Directions: Students may take a copy of the recipe home. They should list the steps in making the clay *in their own words* on the lines below.

Step 1: ____

____

Step 2: ____

____

Step 3: ____

____

Reproducible 4: Connect the Dots

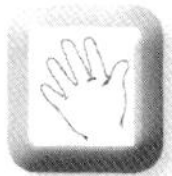

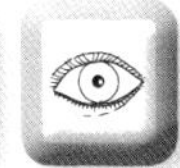

My name is: ______________________________ .

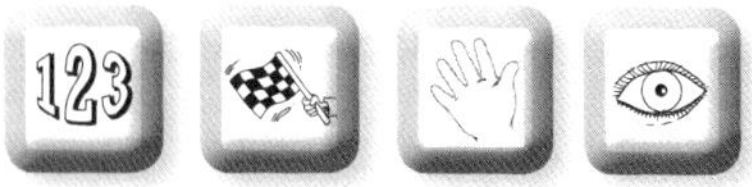

Directions: Connect the dots to create a picture of something that helps us to count the days.

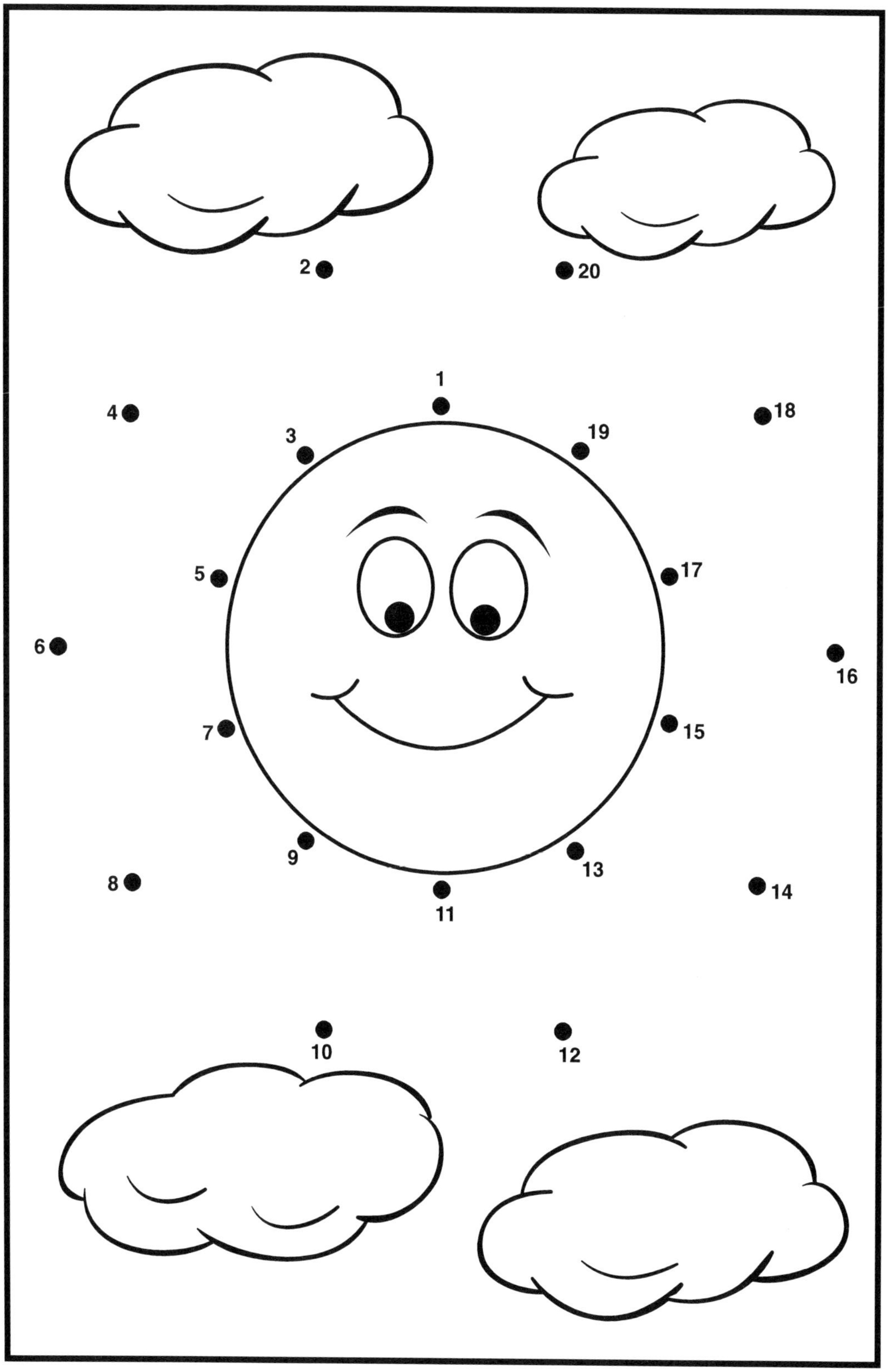

This is a picture of: ____.

Reproducible 5: Writing Numbers

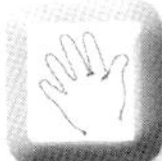

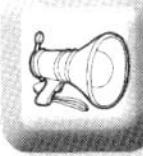

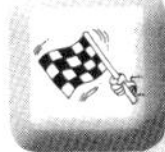

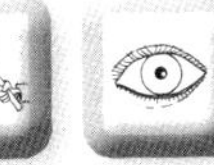

My name is: ______________________________ .

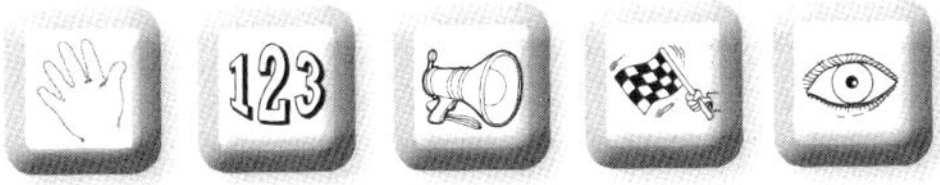

Directions: Trace the numbers 1–10 by counting forward.

1 2 3 4 5

6 7 8 9 10

Now write the numbers 1–10 on the lines below.

Reproducible 6: Writing Numbers

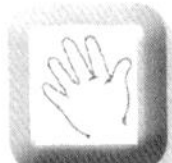

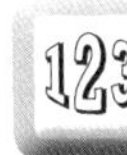

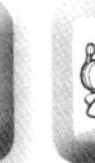

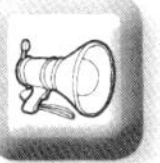

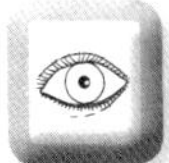

My name is: ______________________________ .

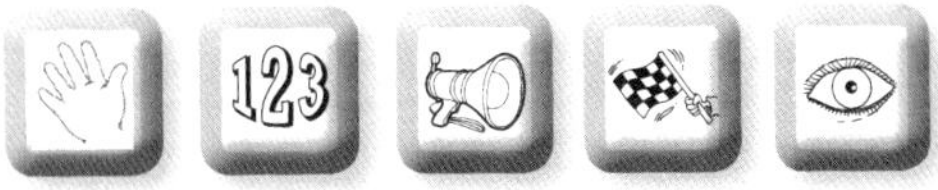

Directions: Trace the numbers 10–1 by counting backward.

10 9 8 7 6

5 4 3 2 1

Now write the numbers 10–1 on the lines below.

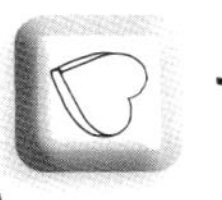

Award Certificate

for

_______________________________________,

Who can now count from 1 to 10

Given on the first day of Spring: _______________

By _________________________________

At _____________________________

Can you count the days til spring?
1 to 10 and everything?
I can do it, fast or slow.
Counting is an important skill to know.

Chapter Five

S Is for Summer Safety:
Thinking About the Sounds of Summer and Being Safe

S is for Summer Safety

S is for the sunshine, warm and damp in June.
It could be a scorcher, 90 degrees by noon.
Be sure to wear your sunscreen, cover head to toe.
Keep your skin protected. Summer is here, you know.

S is for the swimming in the ocean or the pool.
Keeping cool is great, but you should know the rule.
Never swim alone. Always have a friend in tow.
Swimming with friends is safer. Summer is here, you know.

S is for the sailing, out in a raft or boat.
But first secure your life vest to make sure you will float.
The life vest is important, in bright orange or yellow.
It keeps you safe on the water. Summer is here, you know.

S is for the singing around the campfire bright.
But watch your hands and feet when the campfire lights the night.
The fire is for watching or roasting a marshmallow.
Safety around the fire means that summer is here, you know.

S is for the sundaes and the sodas and the snacks.
But make sure you keep them cool or a stomachache will soon attack.
In summer, foods need cooling or you'll soon be feeling low.
Keep your coolers chilled and ready, 'cause summer is here, you know.

S is for staying near your mom or dad or sitters
When you travel to a park or zoo to see the critters.
It is easy to get lost when you are busy and on the go.
So pay attention and listen 'cause summer is here, you know.

S is for snapping your seatbelt every time you get in the car.
It doesn't matter if your trip is near or very far.
The seatbelt keeps you safe if the ride is fast or slow.
Snap up your seatbelt and get ready to ride, 'cause summer is here, you know.

There's so much going on in summer, so much to see and do.
Outside, inside, on water or land, safety is the *S* for you.
Safety for boys and girls and for their parents, too,
Safety in summer makes summer more fun. This is certainly true.

So summer is the season for sunscreen, sand, and sun.
For skating and singing and sodas for everyone.
But take the time for safety, so you will enjoy each day
That June, July, and August send your sunny way.

Brain-Building Activities

Read "S is for Summer Safety" on **page 40** aloud to the children and then ask them to name *S*-words they heard. Record the *S*-words on a chart paper using colored, scented markers.

While reading "S is for Summer Safety" aloud, give the children rhythm instruments to shake when they hear *S*-words. Ask, "Do you hear the sounds of summer?"

Use Reproducible 1: Color by Number, Traced Verse, and Handwriting Practice on **page 43** to develop fine motor and visual discrimination. The children can trace the verse, and then, on the bottom line, copy the verse.

Cut out a large *S*-shape (36 inches) from tag board or bulletin board paper and help the children create a summer safety collage by cutting pictures of summer activities from magazines and gluing them on the *S*.

Play the "What's Wrong with This Story?" game with children by making up little stories about summer activities that have a safety flaw in them. Encourage the children to recognize and describe the flaw. Here is an example:

> "Juan and Julia are excited about helping their Uncle Tito check his crab pots out on the Sound. It is a beautiful June day on the water, and the children can hardly wait to get going. 'Hey, we forgot our life vests,' says Julia as the truck pulls out of the driveway. 'Don't worry about it, let's go,' says Juan."

Follow this up Reproducible 2: Find the Safety Mistakes on **page 44,** in which the children circle what's wrong with the scenes.

Use Reproducible 3: Transparency for Comparing and Contrasting on **page 45** and guide the children in comparing and contrasting summer and winter safety around water, playground, home, outside, on bikes and skates, in the car, and on vacation.

Talk about the five senses. Discuss how we use the senses for protection and to enjoy life. List the senses of taste, touch, sight, smell, and hearing on the board. Ask the children how each sense can help us be safe in the summer.

After the five senses discussion, guide children in tracing their hands on dark blue paper, using chalk or white crayon for contrast. Then, use each finger of the hand to point to a summer safety tip that each sense can help with. For example, one finger might point to a "smell the fire burning" tip. Follow this activity with Reproducible 4: *S* is for Senses on **page 46**.

Make summer safety banners to put up in the school or daycare. Print out a message about summer safety using your computer, and then let the children color and illustrate the banner.

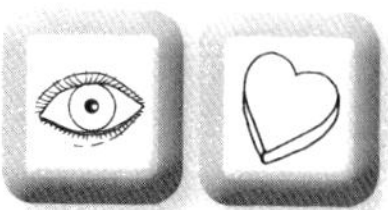

Create spoon puppets using wooden spoons, felt, dry pasta, and other craft materials, and let the children use them to make up a skit about summer safety.

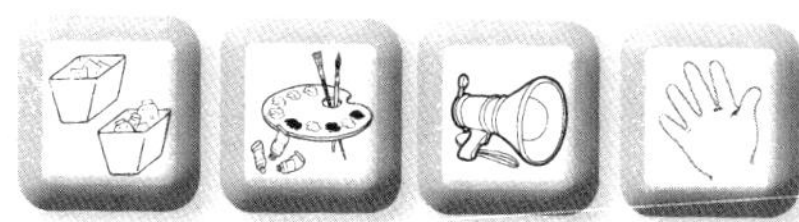

Print out a calendar for each month of summer—June, July, and August— using your computer. Put in important holidays and dates and summer safety tips. Make the calendars into a booklet for each child, and let each student illustrate the boxes with safety tip pictures.

Use Reproducible 5: Summer Safety Maze on **page 47** to practice fine motor skills.

Practice counting and sequencing skills by using Reproducible 6: Connect the Dots on **page 48**.

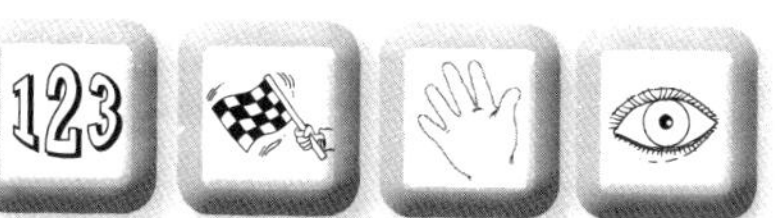

Give each child a piece of white drawing paper that has been folded into a tri-fold, like a brochure. On each page of the tri-fold, help the children write the letter *S* at the top. Then guide the children in illustrating each *S* page with a picture of summer safety that they learned from the *S* is for Summer Safety poem. Reinforce with Reproducible 7: Matching Up Summer Safety on **page 49**.

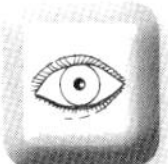    

My name is: ____ .

Color by Number

Directions: Color by number this picture.

1 – yellow
2 – light blue
3 – green
4 – brown
5 – red
6 – black
7 – dark blue

Traced Verse

Directions: Trace the verse.

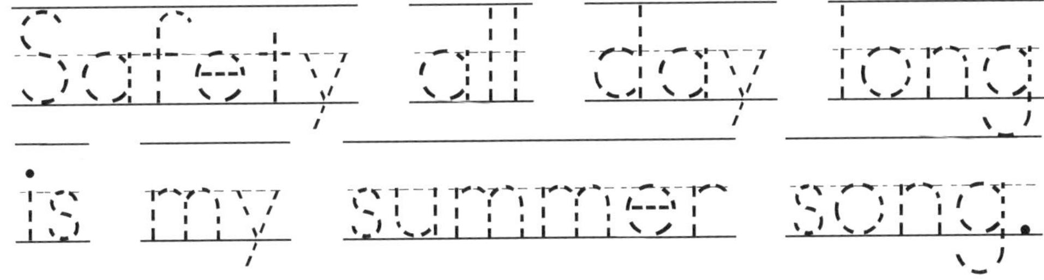

Handwriting Practice

Directions: Now copy the verse on the line below.

Reproducible 2: Find the Safety Mistakes

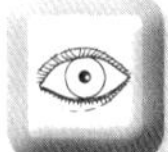

My name is: ______________________________ .

Directions: In this picture, there are five dangerous mistakes that the children are making. Use a red crayon to circle each safety mistake.

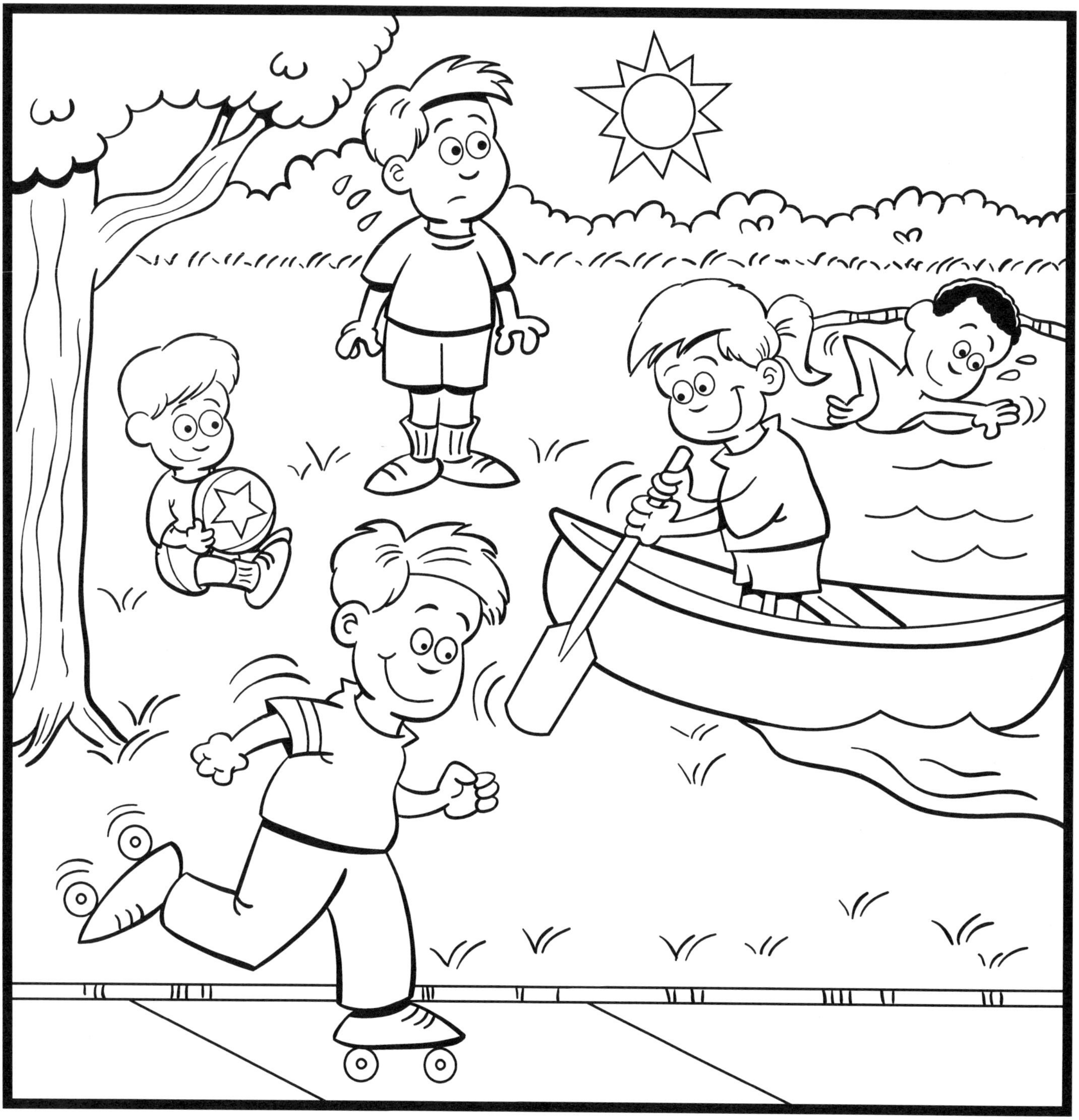

Directions: Write how safety is different in the summer than it is in the winter.

Summer		Winter
	On the water	
	At the playground	
	At home	
	Playing outside	
	On bikes and skates	
	In the car	
	On vacation	

Reproducible 4: S is for Senses

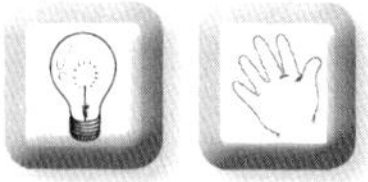

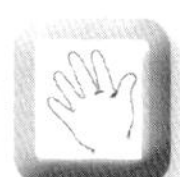

My name is: ________________________________ .

Directions: Look at each picture on the left in which the child is using one of the five senses. Cut out the boxes on the right side of the page and paste the right "sense" next to the picture. Then color the pictures.

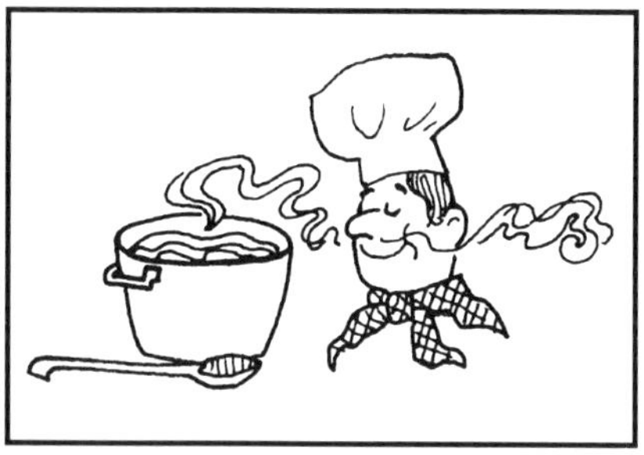

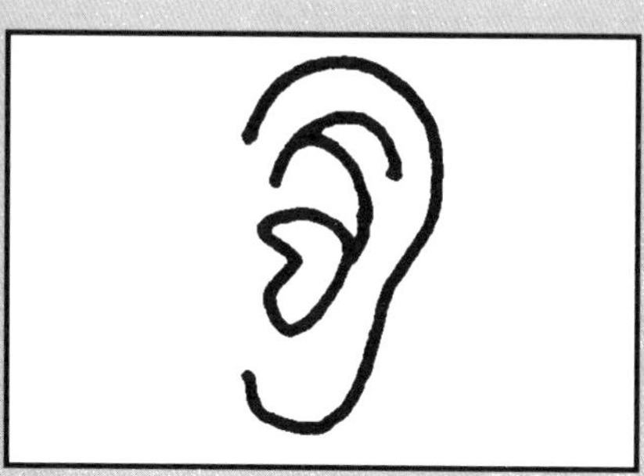

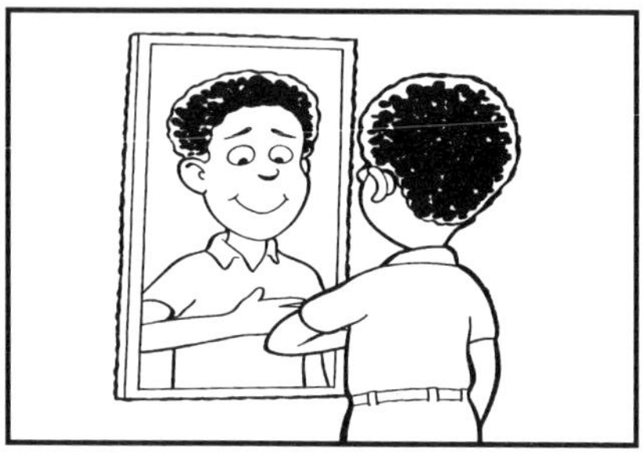

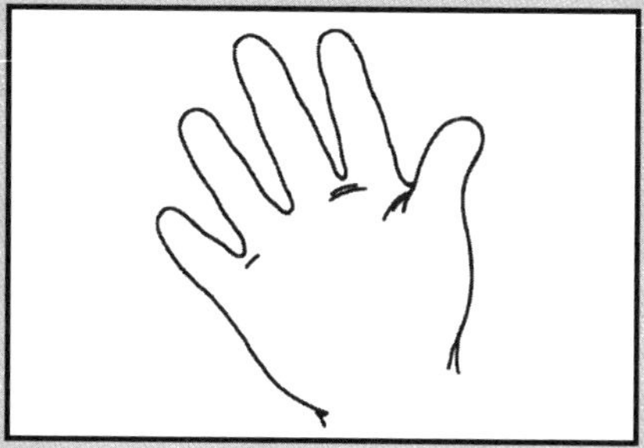

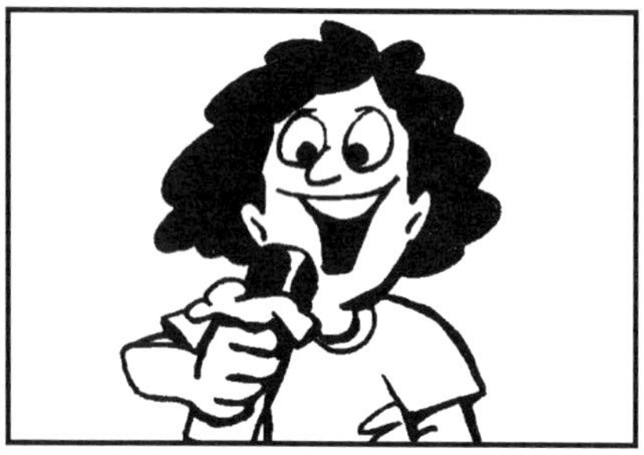

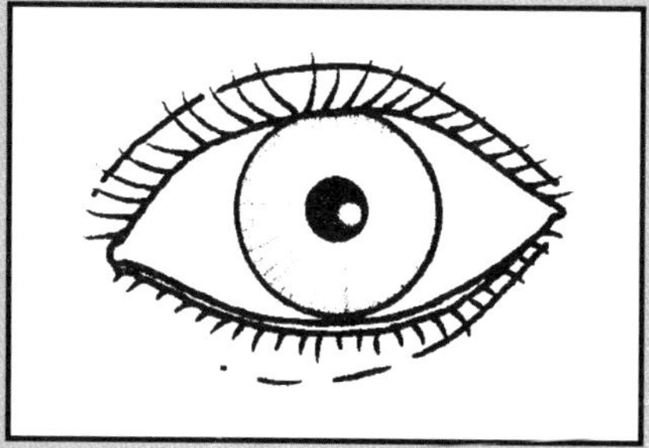

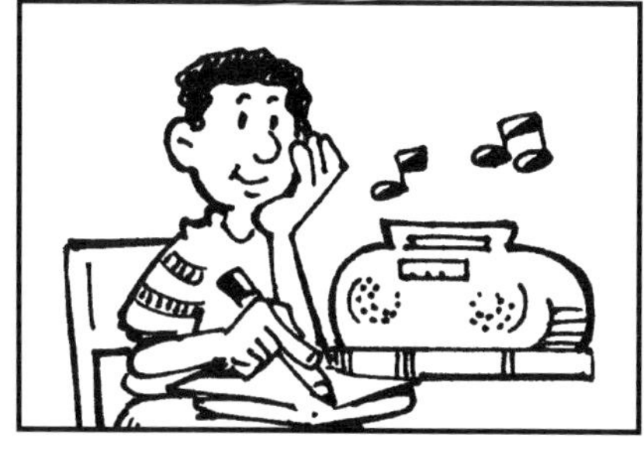

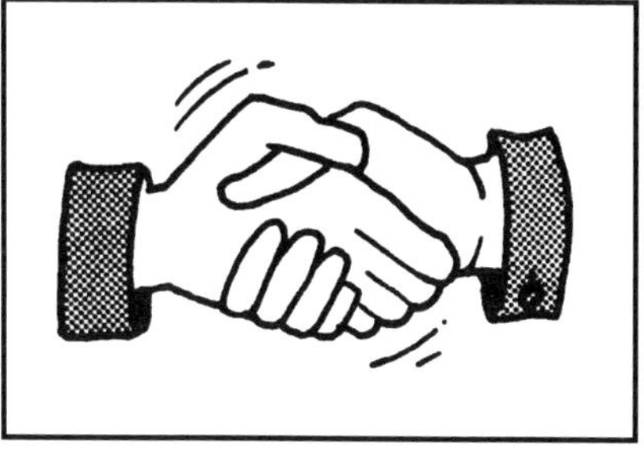

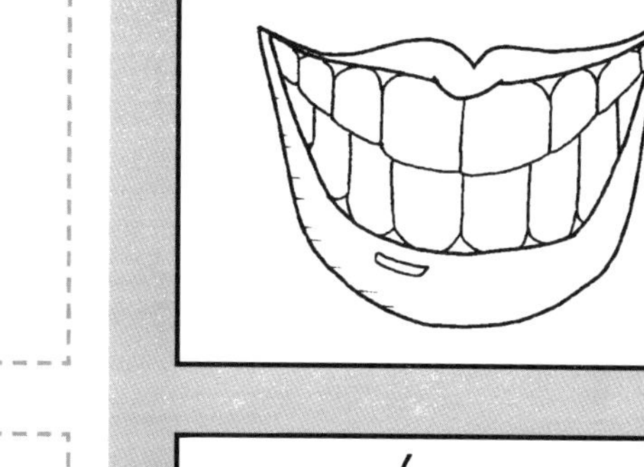

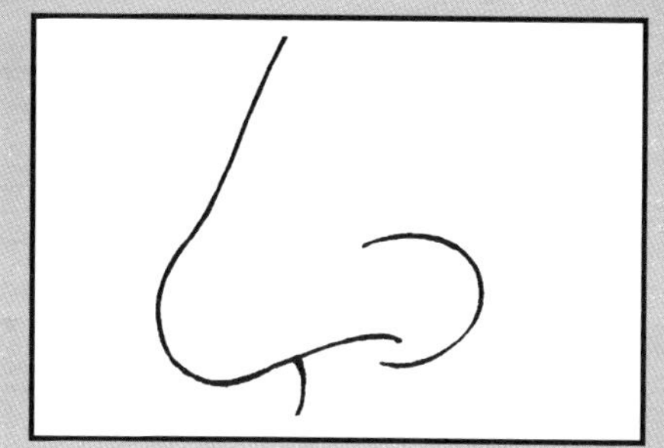

Reproducible 5: Summer Safety Maze

My name is: _______________________________ .

Directions: Put your pencil on the dot that says *Begin*. Find your way to the lifejacket and first aid kit.

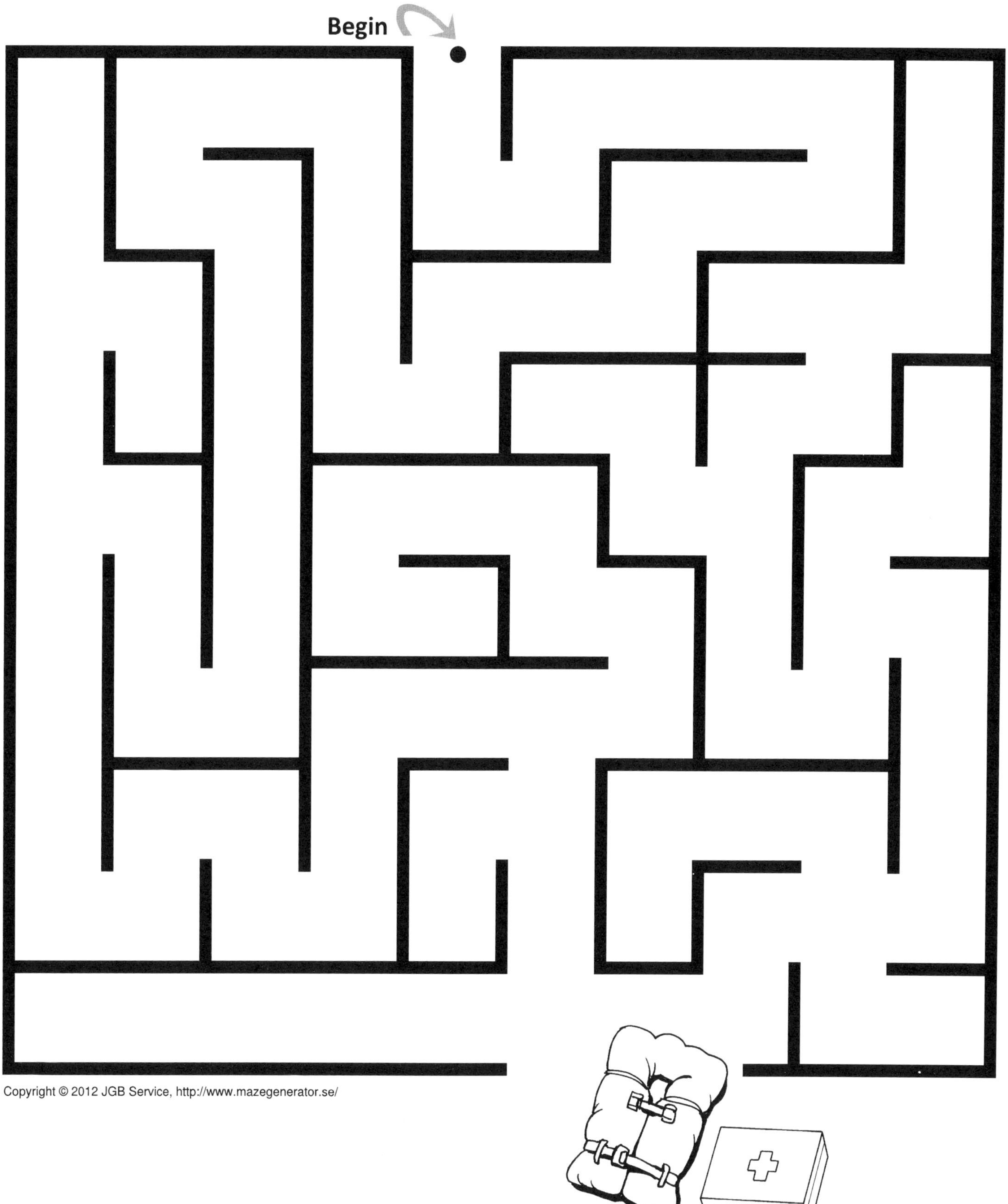

Begin

   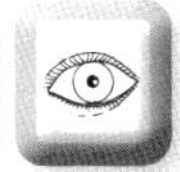

My name is: _______________________________________.

Directions: Place your pencil on the number 1, and connect the dots in order. What picture did you make?

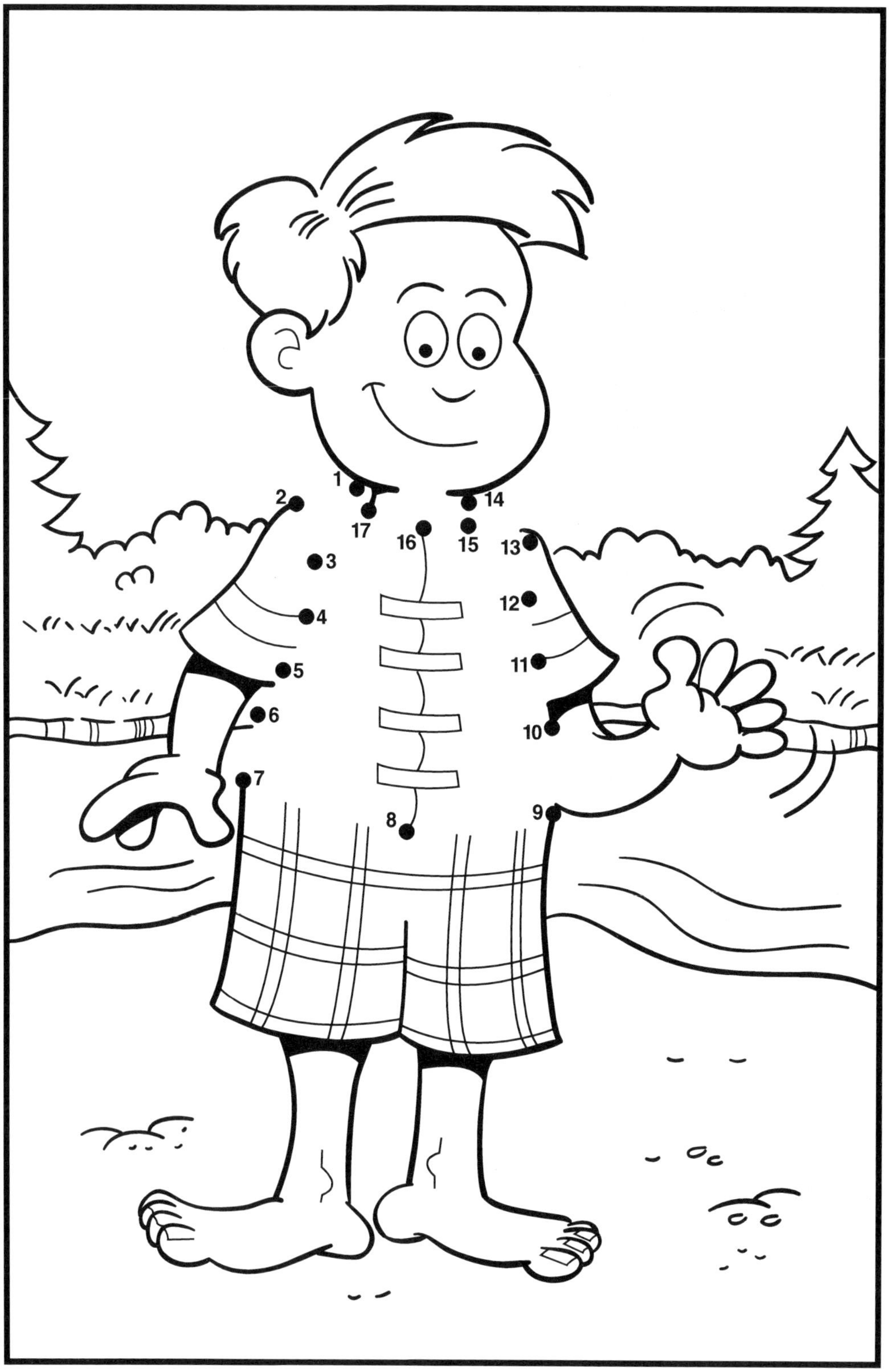

This is a picture of: ____.

    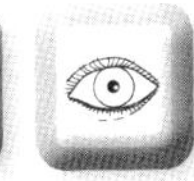

My name is: _________________________________ .

Directions: Draw a line from the summer activity to the safety gear that you need for it.

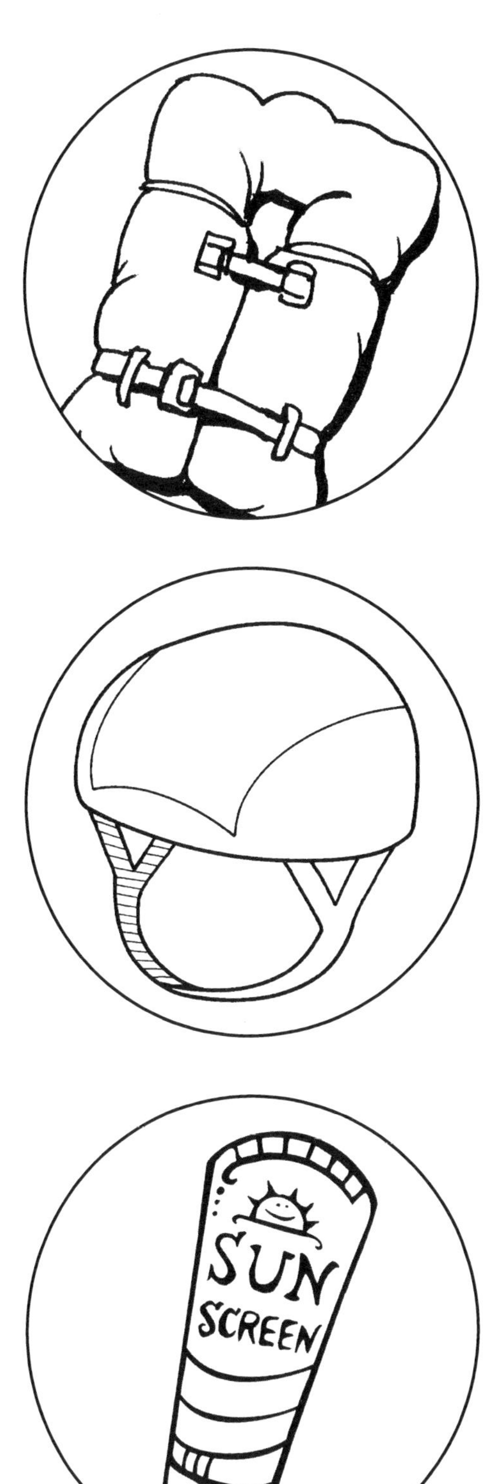

Chapter Six

All Fall Down: Thinking About the First Days of School

All Fall Down

In and out, over, under, all fall down.
Line up for the yellow bus and ride it into town.
School is starting, time for fun,
Your first day of school has now begun.

In and out, over, under, all fall down.
Line up for the yellow bus and ride it into town.
A special class is waiting for you,
With a wonderful teacher to see you through.

In and out, over, under, all fall down.
Line up for the yellow bus and ride it into town.
Meet new friends, see new places,
Lots of laughing, happy faces.

In and out, over, under, all fall down.
Line up for the yellow bus and ride it into town.
Take your turn and don't be rude,
Show a pleasant attitude.

In and out, over, under, all fall down.
Line up for the yellow bus and ride it into town.
Learn to paint, cut and write,
Glue and glitter, what a sight!

In and out, over, under, all fall down.
Line up for the yellow bus and ride it into town.
Counting, cutting, lots to do,
Your brain is getting bigger, too!

In and out, over, under, all fall down.
Line up for the yellow bus and ride it into town.
Instruments and songs to sing,
Making music is a joyful thing.

In and out, over, under, all fall down.
Line up for the yellow bus and ride it into town.
Wear your sweater, grab your lunch,
Don't forget a snack to munch.

In and out, over, under, all fall down.
Line up for the yellow bus and ride it into town.
Learn to share and learn to wait,
Growing up can sure feel great.

In and out, over, under, all fall down.
Line up for the yellow bus and ride it into town.
Telling time and reading words,
Studying nature, plants, and birds.

In and out, over, under, all fall down.
Line up for the yellow bus and ride it into town.
Ride up front, take your seat,
Your school adventure will be neat.

Brain-Building Activities

Make a colorful banner with your class rules printed on them. Keep the rules brief, and include no more than three. Let the children write their names or put their thumb prints (with an ink pad) on the banner.

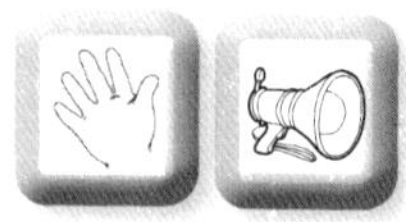

Use paper and scented markers to create a list of places your class will be going into, out of, over to, or under during the year. These prepositions are important in developing proper grammar, and the list helps with verbal fluency.

Use Reproducible 1: Color by Number, Traced Verse, and Handwriting Practice on **page 54** to develop fine motor and visual discrimination. The children can trace the verse, and then, on the bottom line, copy the verse.

Learn the verse and let children create their own movements for a finger play using "All Fall Down" on **page 50**. Add more verses as you teach new concepts.

Tests show that listening skills continue to be a weakness in many children who come to school. Every day, play a game such as lining up by height or sock color. This uses listening to promote thinking and observation. This also works well for transition time.

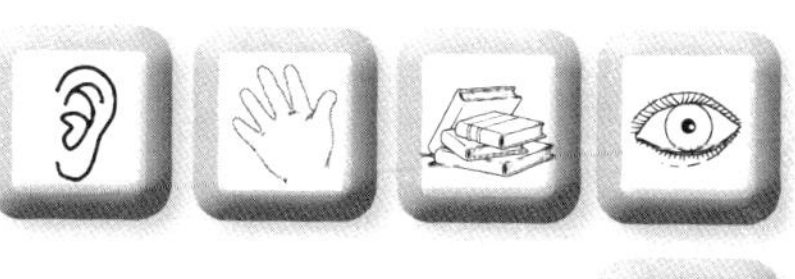

- To complete Reproducible 2 Are You Listening on **page 55**, students should use crayons to follow a set or oral directions that you give. Here is a sample set:

    "Color the child's hair brown and his or her outfit red. Draw a pink flower next to the child."

    "Color the dog brown with black spots."

    "Draw a yellow heart around the rabbit. Give the rabbit pink ears."

    "Color the car green. Make the tires black."

You can use this sheet over and over, changing the directions to build in new skills or longer sentences.

Introduce scissors to the children by having them cut out autumn leaf patterns from Reproducible 3 on **page 56**. Then use a digital camera to take a photo of each child and tape it to the leaf. Use these leaf pictures for door or bulletin board decor that says, "Falling in Love with Kindergarten." The leaves tumble all over the board or door and show off your most beautiful products: the children.

To practice important terms like *in, out, over, under, next to, on,* and *near,* use a playground ball, hoola hoops, and plastic laundry baskets to make an obstacle course. Give oral directions to the children as they move the balls down the course. Example: "Put the ball *IN* the basket. Put the ball *NEAR* the chair." Change directions for each child.

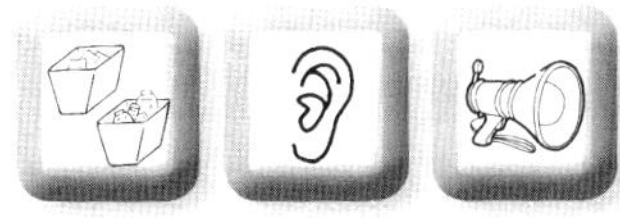

Practice counting and sequencing skills by using Reproducible 4: Connect the Dots on **page 57**.

Do Reproducible 5: Rebus Story on **page 58** to build language and to practice sequencing skills.

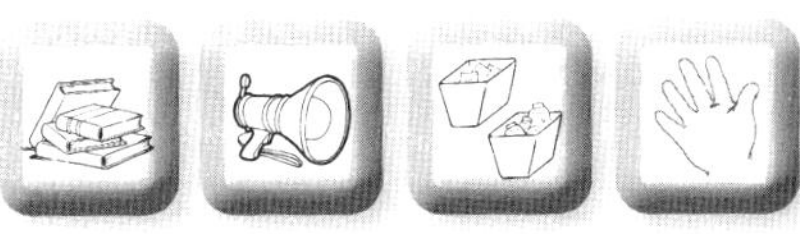

Use all modalities to complete Reproducible 6: Matching Activity on **page 59**.

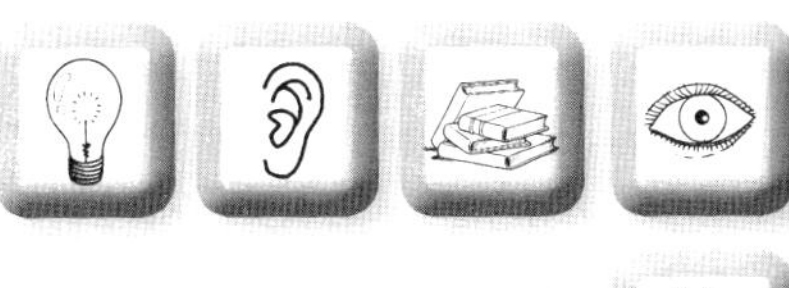

Wrap up this chapter with Reproducible 7: Amazing Autumn Maze on **page 60**.

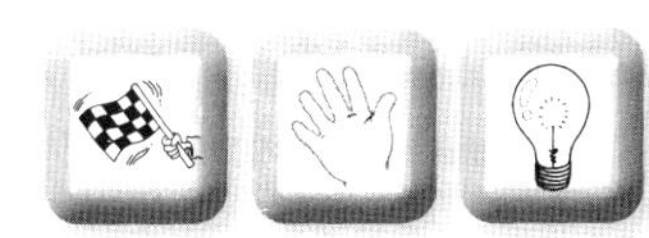

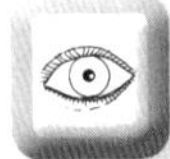    

My name is: ____ .

Color by Number

Directions: Color by number this picture.

1 – red
2 – yellow
3 – brown
4 – green
5 – light blue
6 – peach
7 – gray
8 – orange
9 – dark blue

Traced Verse

Directions: Trace the verse.

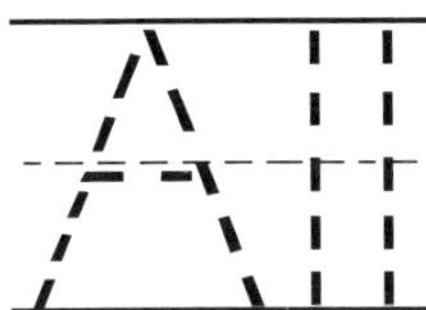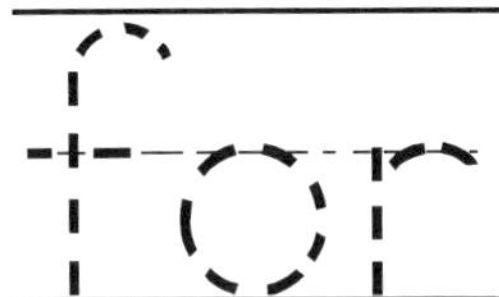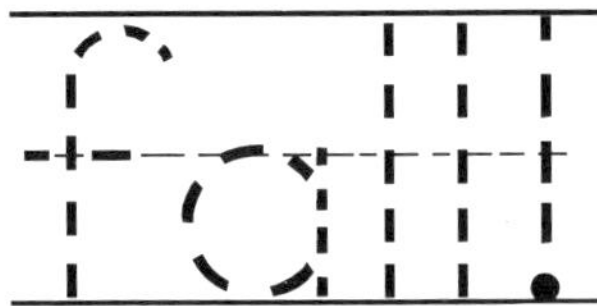

Handwriting Practice

Directions: Now copy the verse on the line below.

____

____

   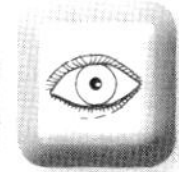

My name is: ___________________________ .

Directions: Listen as your teacher reads the directions, and use your crayon to place the correct items in each box.

Reproducible 3: Autumn Leaf Pattern for the Picture Frame

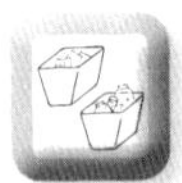

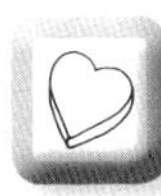

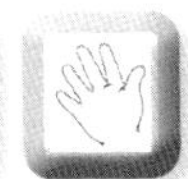

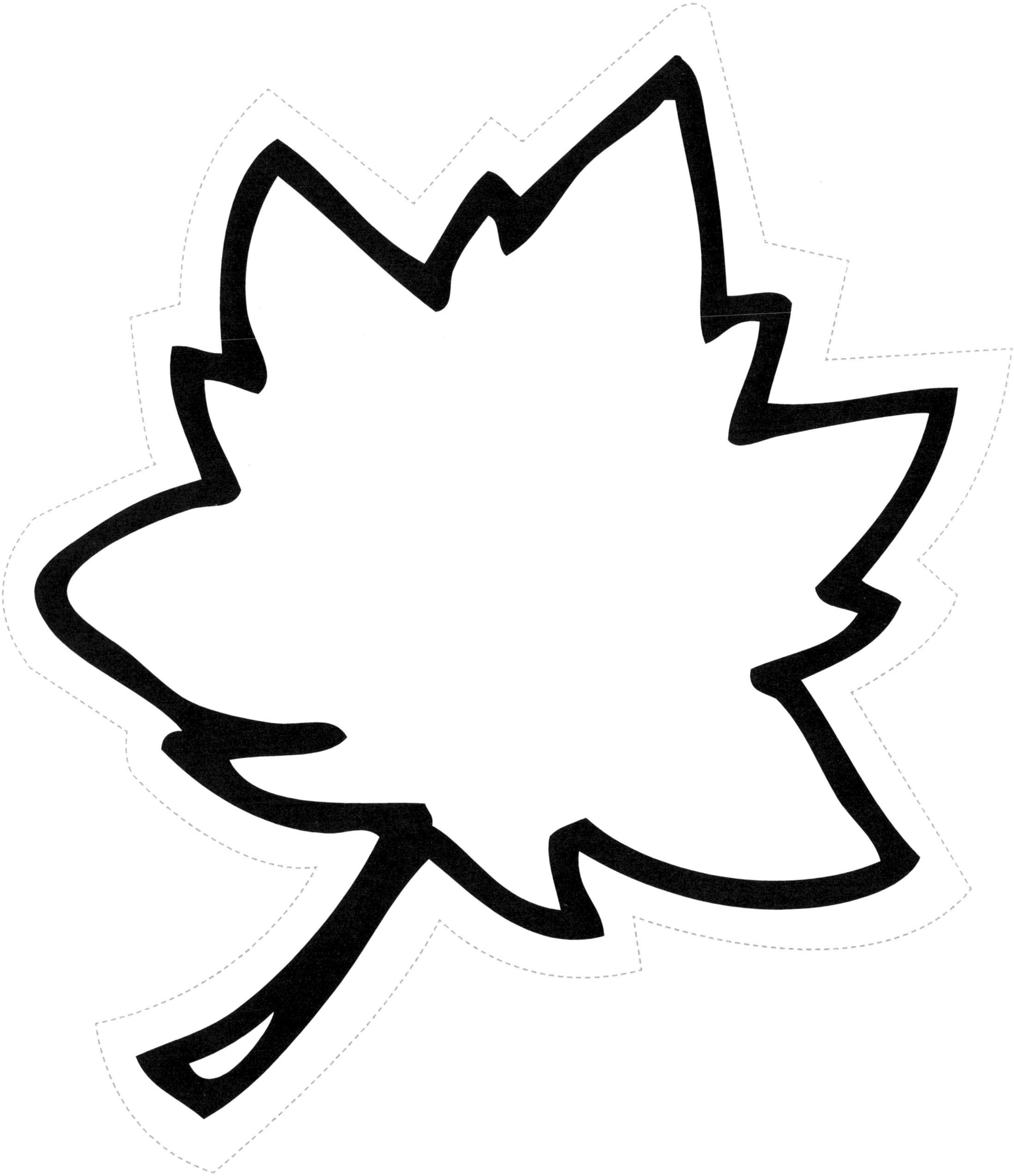

Reproducible 4: Connect the Dots

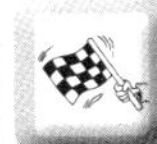

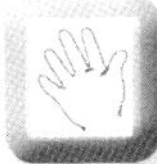

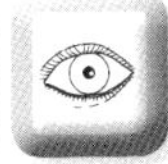

My name is: ______________________________ .

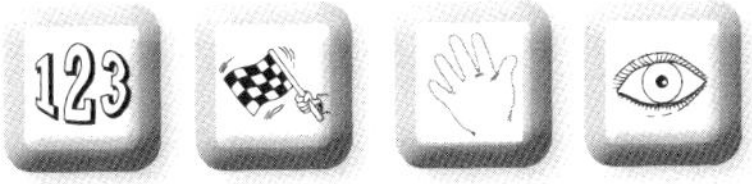

Directions: Put your pencil on the number 1 and connect the dots in order. What picture did you make?

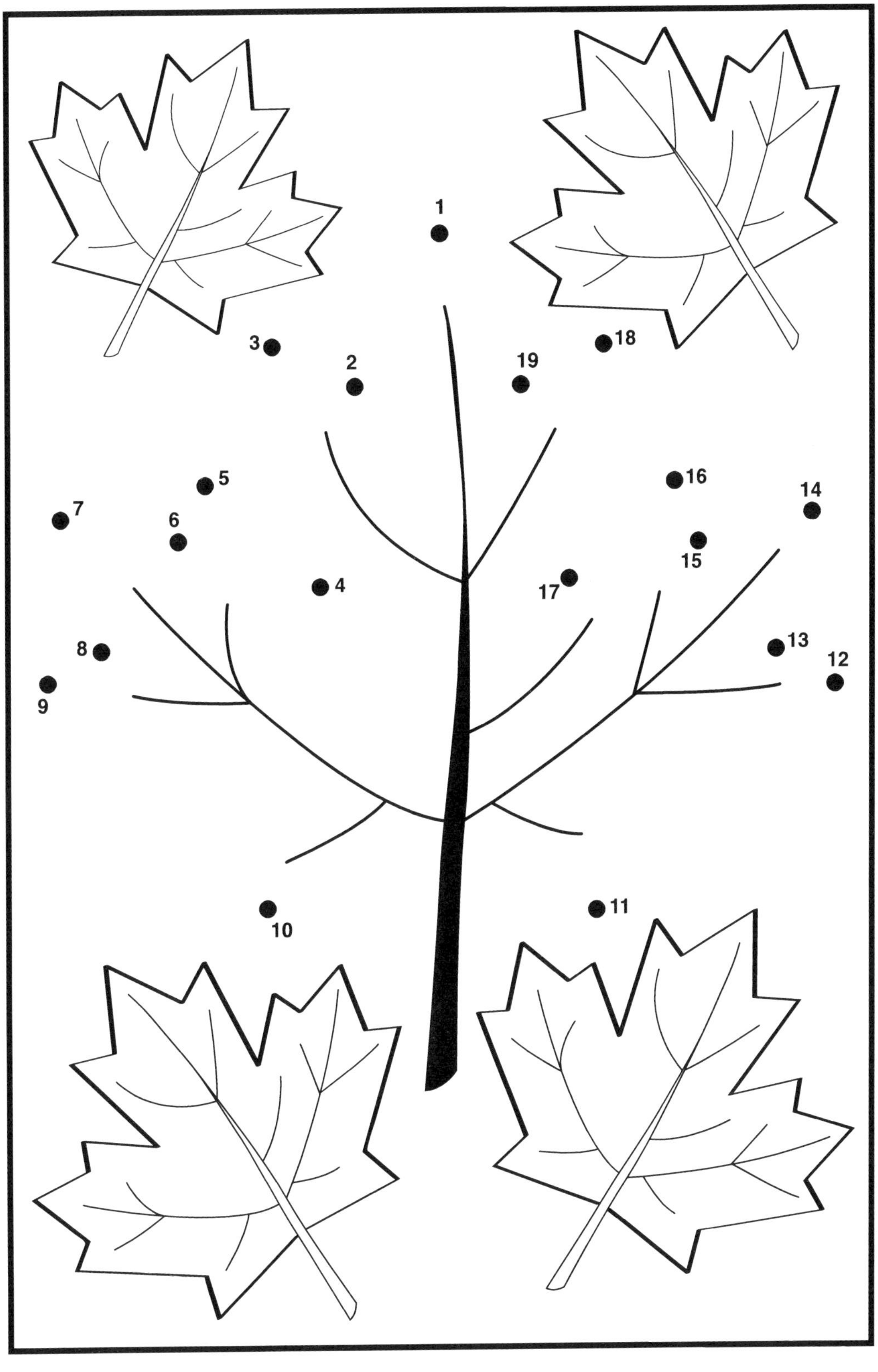

This is a picture of: ____.

My name is: _______________________________.

Directions: Cut out the picture boxes at the bottom of the page. Paste the pictures into the story where they belong. Read your story to a friend.

In fall, the [ ] come off the  .

We like to [ ] the [ ] into a big

. Then we [ ] .

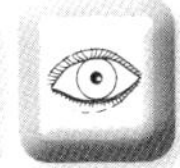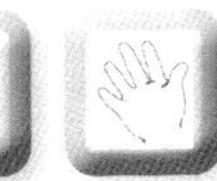

My name is: ________________________________ .

Directions: Draw a line to match the picture and the word.

bus

art

lunch

book

   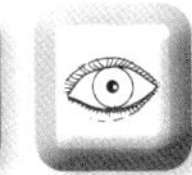

My name is: _________________________________ .

Directions: Place your pencil on the dot that says *Begin*, and find the shortest, clear path to the pile of leaves that the children have raked.

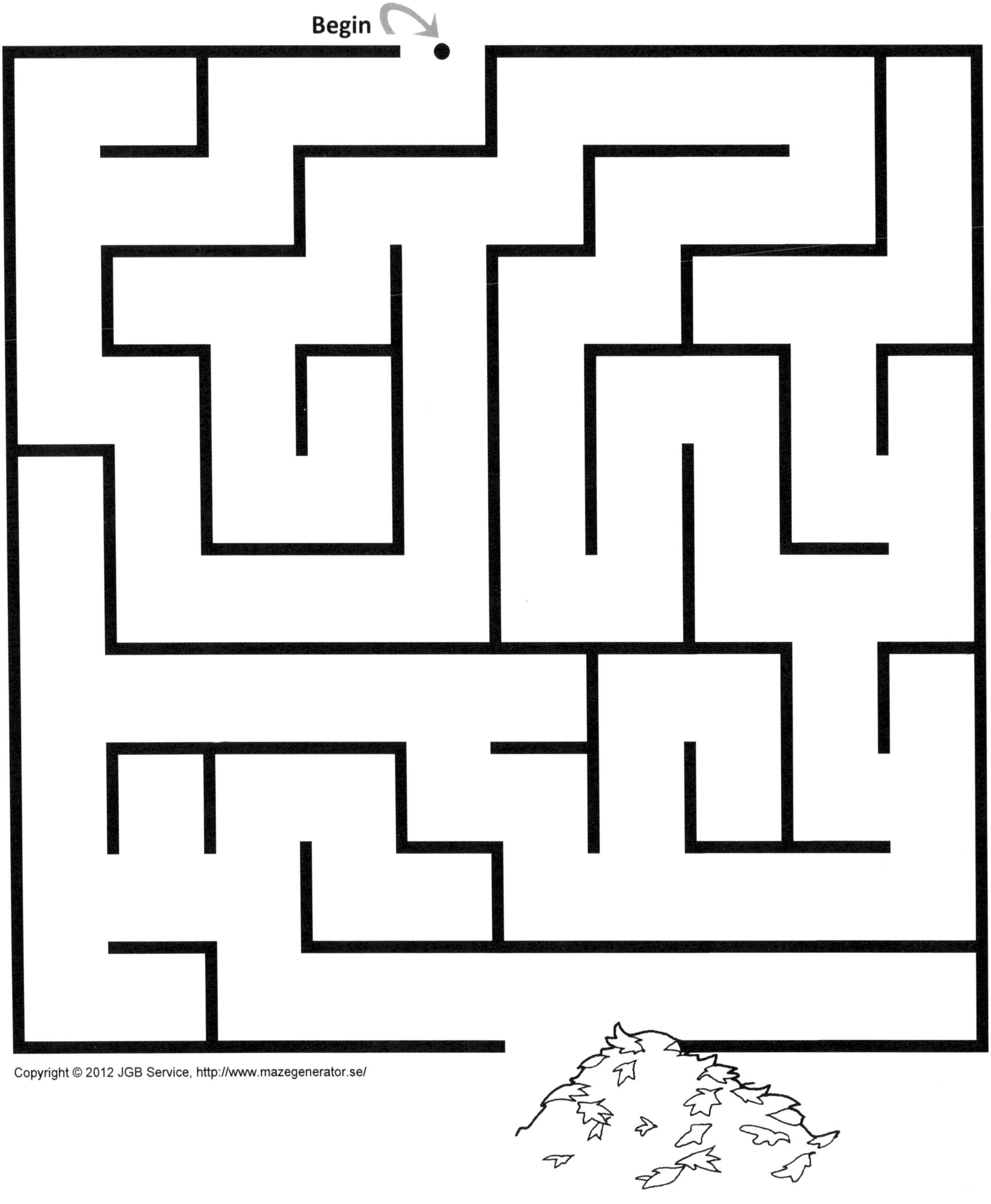

Begin

60

# Chapter Seven
Wonderful Winter Words: Thinking About Cold Things

Wonderful Winter Words

Cold, colder, coldest,
Winter winds blow the boldest.
Whipping up Fahrenheit or Celsius,
Winter winds are freezing us!

Slick, slicker, slickest,
Winter ponds freeze the quickest.
For skating and sliding fast and free,
Too much fun for you and me!

Freeze, frozen, freezing,
Winter snows are never teasing.
At 32 degrees the rain turns to snow,
Sprinkling the earth in a white, puffy show.

Short, shorter, shortest,
Winter days give the sun a rest.
Then in late December, the shortest day of all,
When the winter solstice comes to call.

Deep, deeper, deepest,
Bulbs snuggle in for a winter's rest.
Waiting for the warmth of spring to come,
And beckon them to reach for the sun.

Thick, thicker, thickest,
Winter icicles are slickest.
Shining and sparkling like diamonds or stars,
Hanging like jewels from buses and cars.

Sweet, sweeter, sweetest,
A cup of chocolate tastes the best.
When your hands are cold and the day is
bleak,
And your teeth are chattering so hard you
can't speak.

Sick, sicker, sickest,
A winter cold flutters in your nose and chest.
With a cough and sneeze and a fever, too,
Time for a cup of mom's special brew!

Burn, burner, burning,
The logs in our fire are turning.
Golden, orange, glowing red,
Warming our bodies from toes to head.

Chill, chilly, chilling,
Winter days are quickly spilling.
Over December, January, February, too,
Until this chilly season is through!

Brain-Building Activities

After reading "Wonderful Winter Words" aloud, invite children to identify the similarities and differences in sets of words, such as COLD-COLDER-COLDEST. Introduce the concepts of *root words* and *endings*. Ask the children to describe the differences and similarities in both the *structure* (how the words look on paper) and the *meaning* (how the words are used).

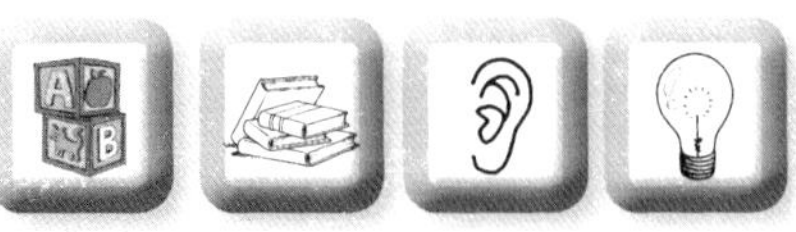

Divide the children into small groups to illustrate a "Big Book" of the poem. Record a stanza on different pages using poster board or large sheets of drawing paper, then give the children markers and stickers to illustrate the pages. Use shower curtain rings to bind the book together.

Use magazines to make collages of winter things, such as cups of hot soup, snowmen, and pictures of people in warm clothing. As the children select, cut, and paste their pictures, engage them in conversation about why the objects or pictures are categorized as wintry.

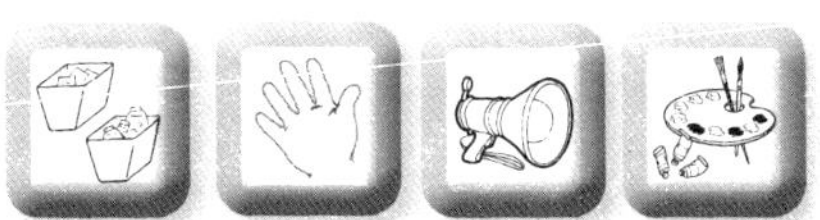

Use Reproducible 1: Color by Number, Traced Verse, and Handwriting Practice on **page 64** to develop fine motor and visual discrimination. The children can trace the verse and then on the bottom line, copy the verse.

To improve word recognition skills in the beginning reader, complete Reproducible 2: Rebus Story on **page 65**.

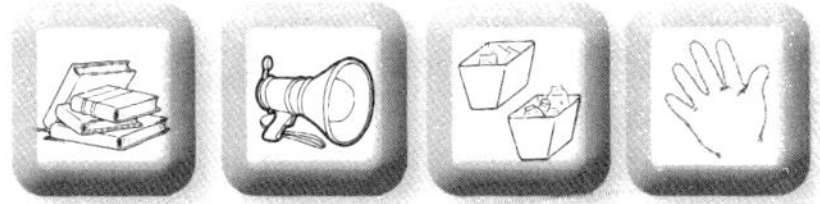

Practice using the calendar to mark off the days in the school year. Put the months into seasonal groups, such as December, January, and February (winter months) or March, April, and May (spring months). It is a good idea to print each set of months on separate, color-coded pages: yellow for summer, blue for winter, green for spring, and orange for autumn.

Use manipulatives such as animal crackers to illustrate simple greater-and-less story problems. For example, give each child a plastic cup with animal crackers in it. Ask students to use the crackers to show the math problem *3 is more than 1*.

Introduce concepts such as *heavy, heavier, heaviest*, and *light, lighter, lightest* by weighing simple objects with a kitchen scale. Show children how to record their data on a chart. This is how we begin to teach the science process skill of recording data. Use Reproducible 3: Transparency for Weight Data on **page 66** for recording data.

Use rhythm instruments to make a sound when the children hear either a pair of rhyming words or a set of superlatives (warm, warmer, warmest).

To develop visual memory and sequencing skills, let the children complete Reproducible 4: Put the Story in Order on **page 67**. The task is to cut out the four pictures and put them in sequential order.

Help children build fine motor skills by having them complete Reproducible 5: Wonderful Winter Maze on **page 68**.

Have children complete Reproducible 6: Connect the Dots on **page 69** for manual dexterity as well as counting and sequencing skills.

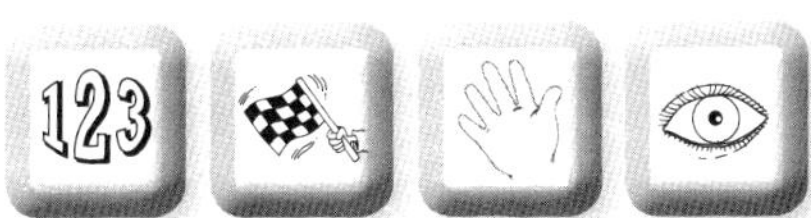

Chill cans of shaving cream (menthol is refreshing). Spread the shaving cream out on old shower curtains laid on the floor. Invite the children to "paint snow pictures."

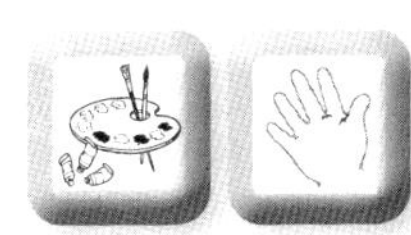

Build vocabulary and schema for winter by having the children complete Reproducible 7: Listening for Winter Words on **page 70**.

Make get-well cards using fabric, glitter, stickers, and other simple materials, and share them with other teachers, children, and school workers who are suffering with winter colds or the flu. Discuss why making and giving a simple card could help someone feel better even though the card does not contain medicine.

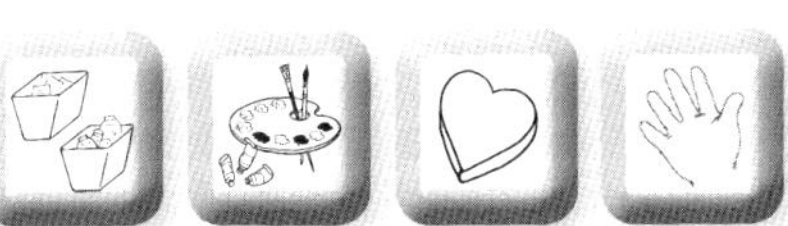

My name is: ___________________________ .

Directions: Color by number this picture.

1 – red
2 – purple
3 – brown
4 – orange
5 – green
6 – light blue
7 – dark blue
8 – yellow
9 – black
10 – peach

Traced Verse

Directions: Trace the verse.

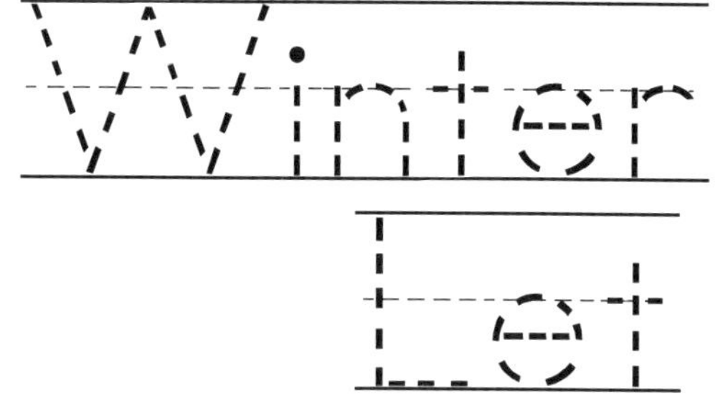

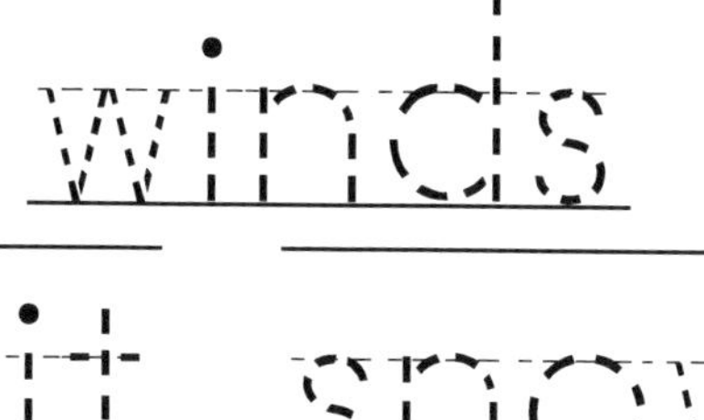
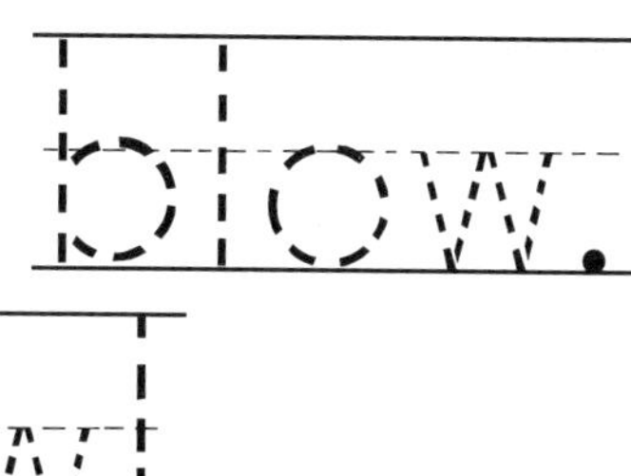

Handwriting Practice

Directions: Now copy the verse on the line below.

   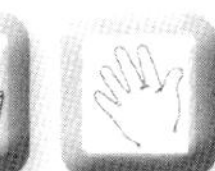

My name is: ________________________________ .

Directions: Cut out the picture boxes at the bottom of the page. Paste the pictures into the story where they belong. Read your story to a friend.

It is [ ] in winter. We put on warm [ ]

and [ ] . Then we go out to play in the [ ] .

We make a [ ] . He has a [ ] on top.

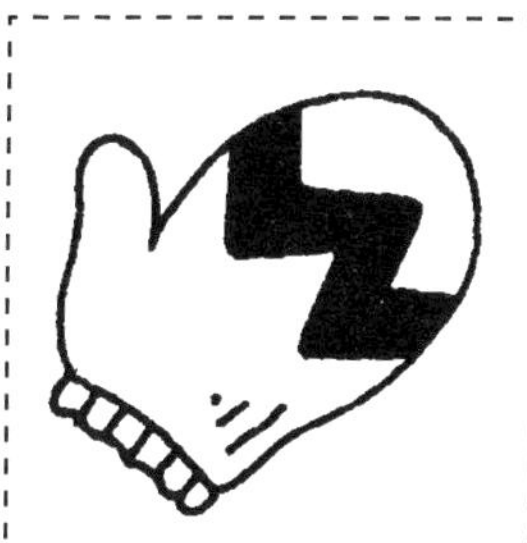

My name is _________________________________ .

Recording Data in ____________________'s Class

Objects We Weighed	Weight in Ounces	**Finding** (Heavy, Heavier, Heaviest, orLight, Lighter, Lightest)
pencil		
chalk		
crayon		
block		
puzzle piece		
scissors		
mitten		
glove		
hat		
stick of gum		
penny		
dollar bill		

My name is _______________________________________ .

Directions: Look at the pictures below. They tell a story. Cut the pictures out. Color them. Write the numbers 1 to 6 in the boxes in the corner of each picture to show the order of events.

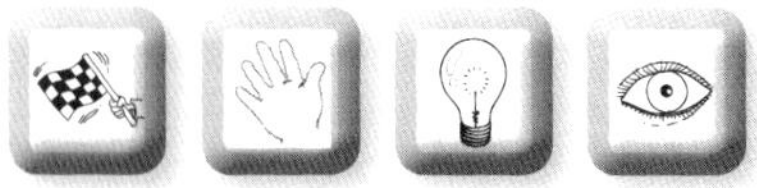

   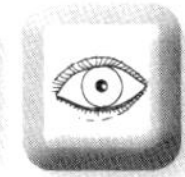

My name is _________________________________ .

Directions: Place your pencil on the dot that says *begin*, and find the shortest, clear path to the snowman. At the bottom of the page, complete the sentence with a word that you choose.

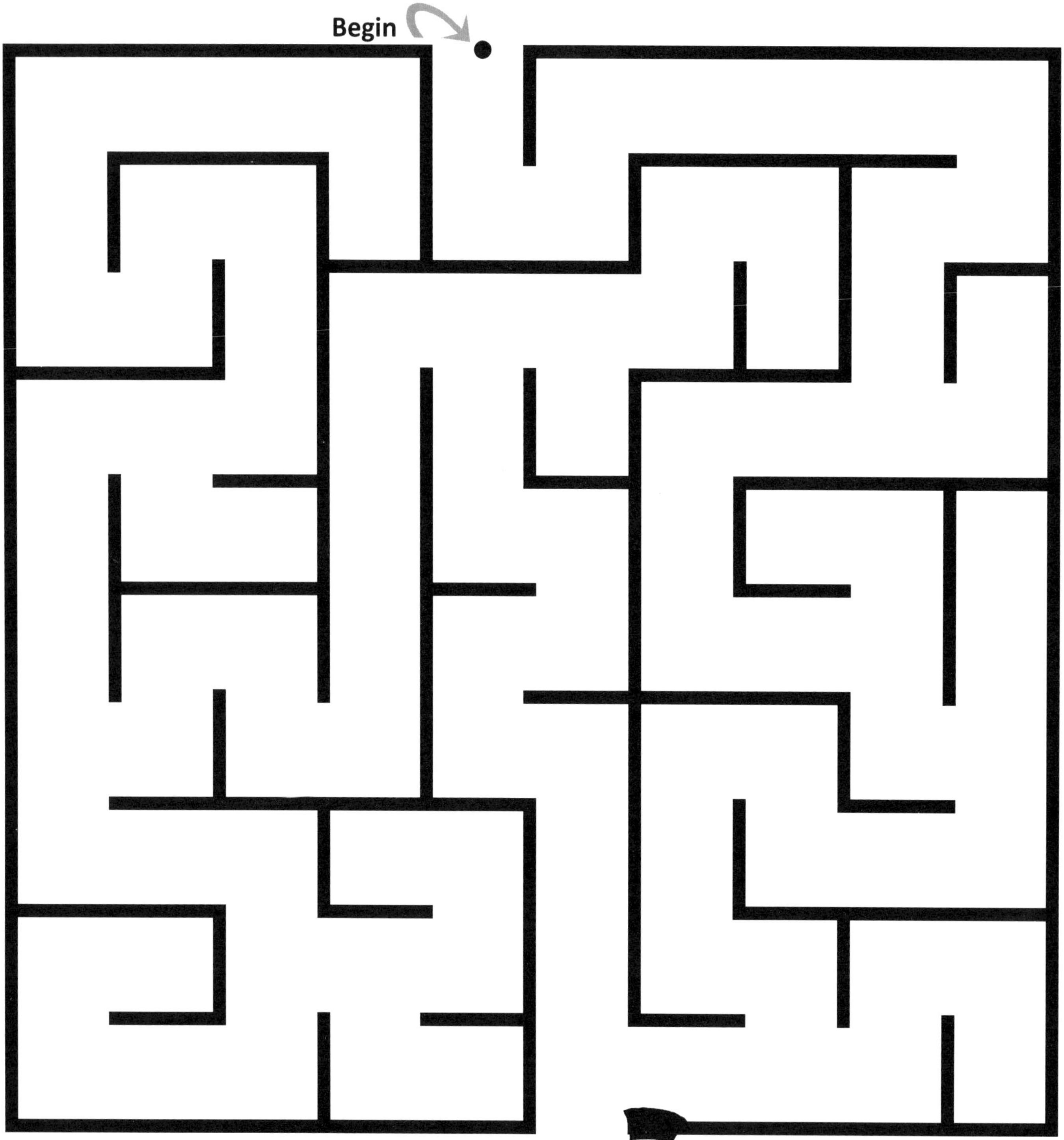

Begin

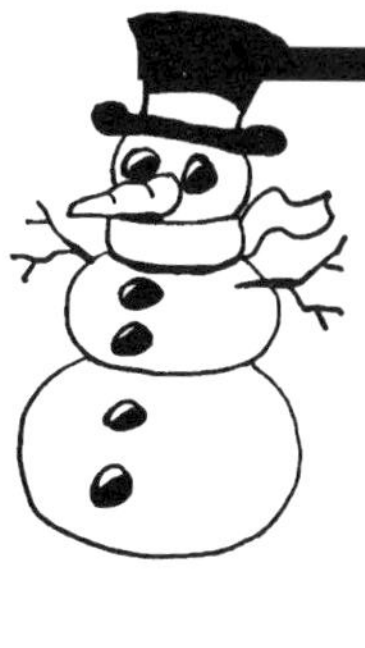

Snow is very_____________________________.

Reproducible 6: Connect the Dots

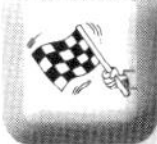

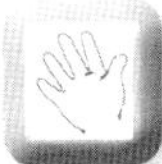

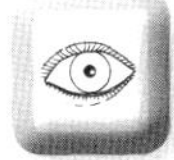

My name is: ______________________________ .

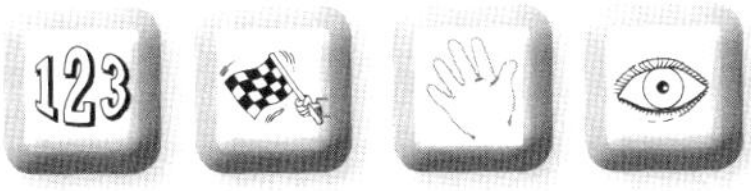

Directions: Place your pencil on the number 1 and connect the dots in order. What picture did you make?

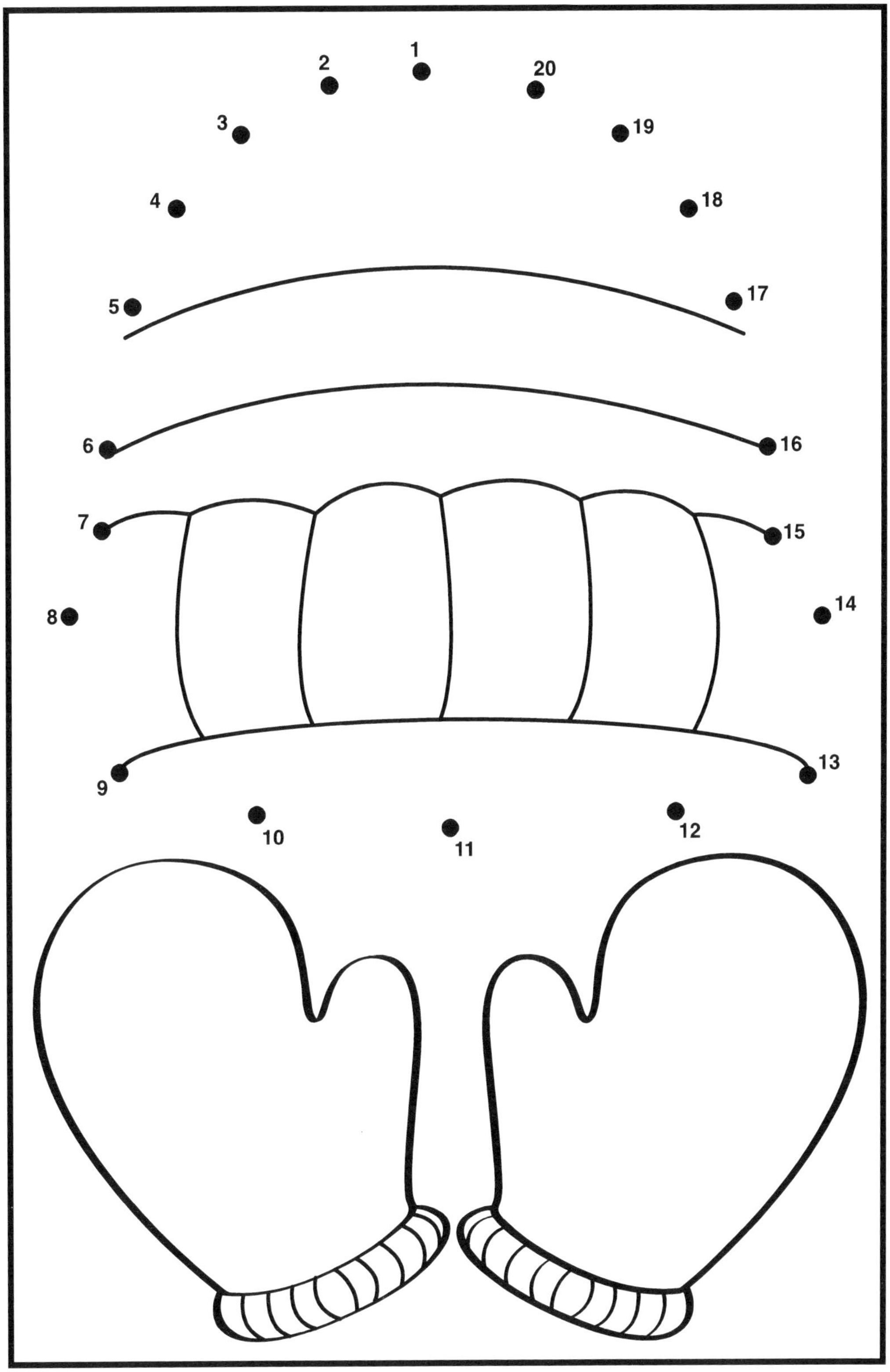

This is a picture of: ____.

Reproducible 7: Listening for Winter Words

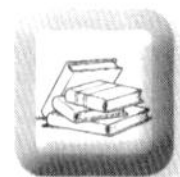

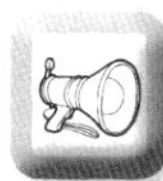

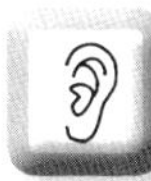

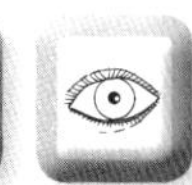

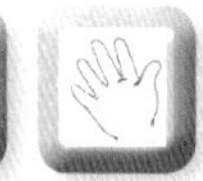

My name is: ______________________ .

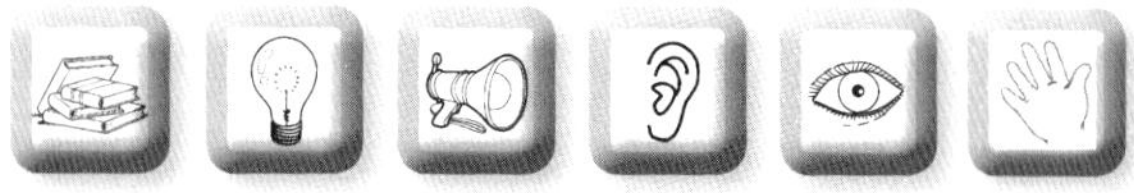

Directions: Circle the picture if it contains something you see in winter. Write the word **winter** under the pictures you circled.

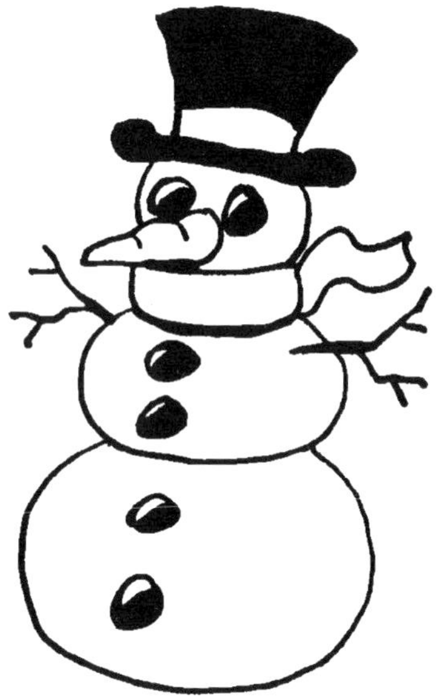

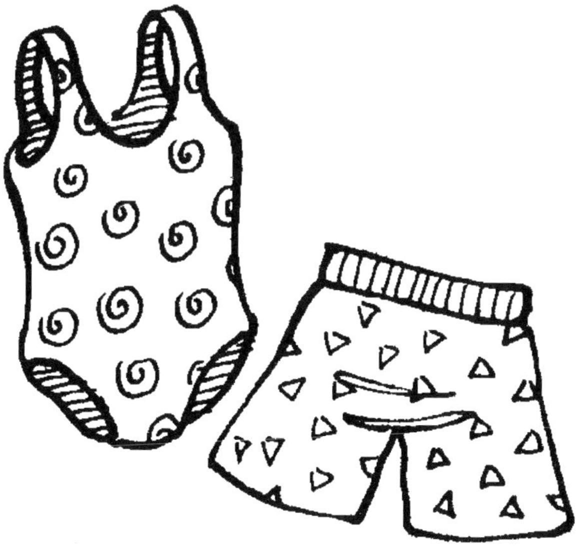

____

____

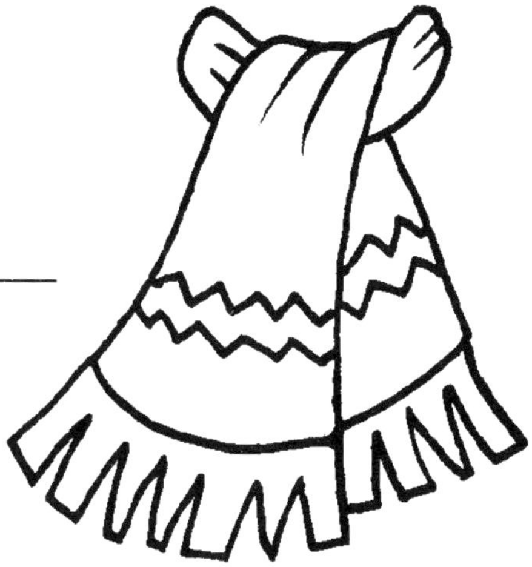

____

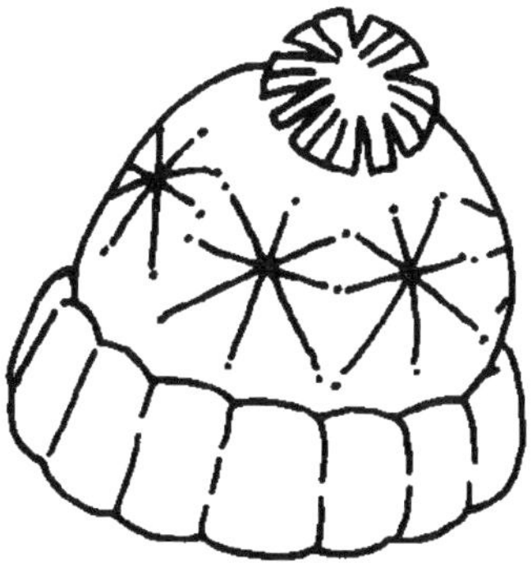

____

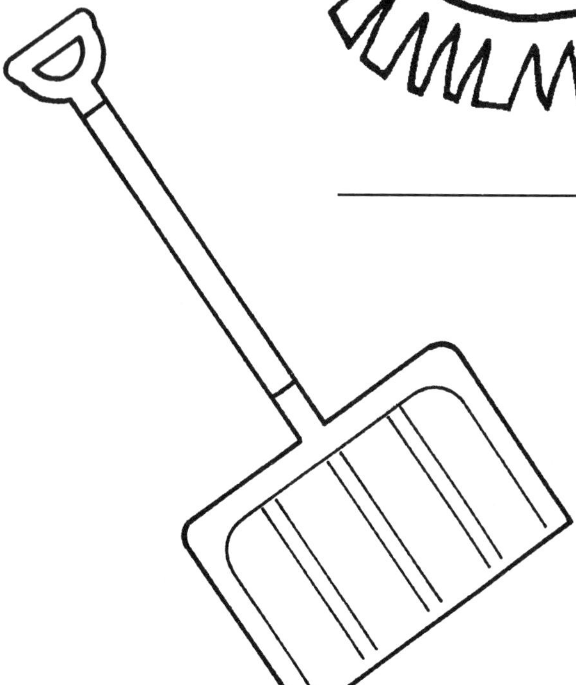

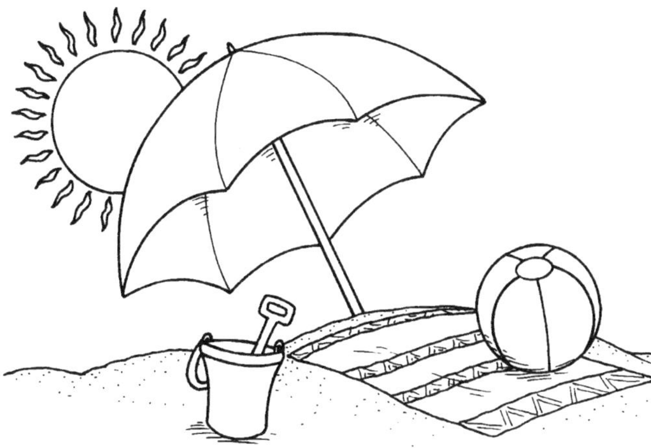

____

____

 Chapter Eight

Hooray for the 100th Day!
Celebrating a Milestone in the School Year

Hooray for the 100th Day

Hooray, hooray! It's the 100th Day!
The school year is skipping merrily away.
But today we take the time to say
It's been fun in 100 different ways.

We have had 100 greetings to share.
"Hello, how are you? Hey, what's going on down there?"
We have had 100 outfits to wear,
And 100 different looks for our hair.

We ate 100 lunches and snacks,
And carried 100 loads of backpacks
To a class where our teacher wore 100 smiles
In spite of our hundreds of troubles and trials.

100 kinds of weather to show
Clouds and sun and winds that blow.
As the fall and winter come and go,
And hundreds of tides ebb and flow.

100 stories to read on the rug,
And 100 days of jump rope to pull and tug.
100 friends to tease or hug
Or play with on the grass like a scampering bug.

100 chances to slip down the slide,
And 100 turns on the merry-go-ride.
100 games to run and hide,
Or call "Red Rover" to the other side.

100 lessons, so much to know,
Taking our brains where they want to go.
Getting smarter and faster, you know,
100 kids with so much to show.

As every day of the hundred went by,
We learned how to think and do and try.
To reach up high, as far as the sky,
"I can do it" the children cry.

The teachers are proud and the parents are, too.
We can name our colors, red and blue,
Say our phone numbers, tie our shoes,
And sing the alphabet all the way through.

It takes 100 days to learn to write
And do your home-reading every night,
To learn to button your jacket up tight,
And learn how to share and not to fight.

So we bring in our hundreds of trinkets and caps,
Hundreds of pasta shapes and bottle top snaps,
100 candies and baseball team caps,
And 100 envelopes with 100 flaps.

In all of the classes all of the kids
With hundreds of bottles and baskets and lids
Lined up their goodies to count and admire
Wearing 100-day t-shirts, our special attire.

The nicest thing about the 100th day
Is the fact that school is here to stay.
Through the rest of winter and into spring,
We can think and learn and laugh and sing.

Brain-Building Activities

Have children use Reproducible 1: Color by Number, Traced Verse, and Handwriting Practice on **page 75** to develop fine motor and visual discrimination. The children can *trace the verse,* and then, on the bottom line, copy the verse.

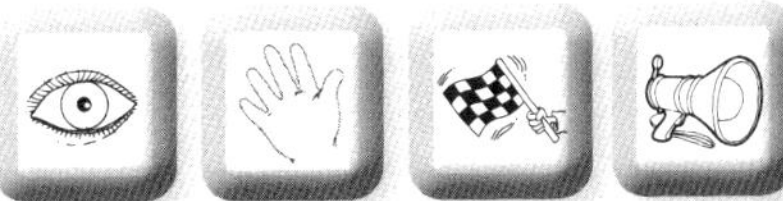

Create a "Number Words" book with the children. Using magazines, scissors, glue, and booklets that follow the format of Reproducible 2: Make a Number Book on **pages 76 - 81**, instruct children to cut out pictures of objects to match the number and number word for each page. For example, on the page that has Five (5) on the top, a child might cut out five dogs or five cookies to paste on the page.

After reading "Hooray for the 100th Day" on **pages 71 - 72** aloud, ask the children how they have changed during these first 100 days of school. For example, ask if they have learned to be kind or to share or to be patient. Record the children's responses on chart paper, and then guide them in completing Reproducible 3: Five Ways in 100 Days on **page 82**. This activity helps children to articulate their feelings.

Create a "Marvelous Math Words" collage by providing small groups with printed materials such as magazines, newspapers, and grocery store circulars, a sheet of poster board, scissors, and glue. Ask the children to use a red felt pen to circle any number words or numbers used with words in the printed pages. The children need not be able to read all the material, just recognize the numbers or number words. After identifying their finds and sharing them with the group, the teams cut out the words and numbers and glue them in attractive designs on the poster board entitled "Marvelous Math Words."

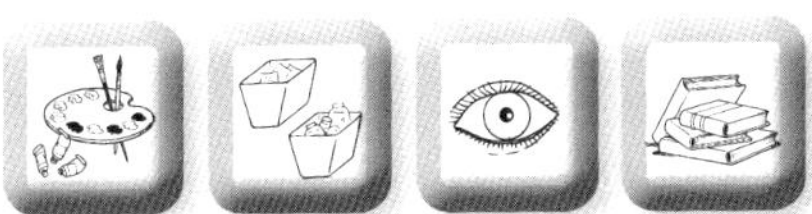

Celebrate on the 100th day of school by setting up a display of "100 Items" that children bring in. Make sure the items are visible and portable—for example, 100 jelly beans in a clear jar, 100 bottle caps linked together, or 100 pieces of pasta on a thread.

Seat groups of children at worktables with four or five children in each group. Give each group 100 pieces of cereal or candy in a dish and ask them to figure out how to share them equally. Discuss the concept of *equal.*

Encourage scientific observation and analysis by asking children to compare different groups of 100 items. Use Reproducible 4: Is 100 Always the Same? on **page 83**; you can insert items from your own 100th day celebration.

Using simple jingle bells from a craft store, let the children create handmade bells by stringing bells onto ribbon or yarn. Give the children 100 bells to string in different groupings. After creating the bells, give the children an opportunity to play the bells fast, slowly, softly, briskly, etc. Ask this question each time: "How do 100 bells sound?"

This activity has two parts: preparing the materials and making the pictures. Using popcorn, pasta, or dried beans (or combinations of each), give children the opportunity to create designs using 100 items. The children must first count out their items into a pie plate or cup, then glue or paste them onto dark paper in a design or scene. Display the artwork under a banner entitled "How Many Ways Do We See 100?"

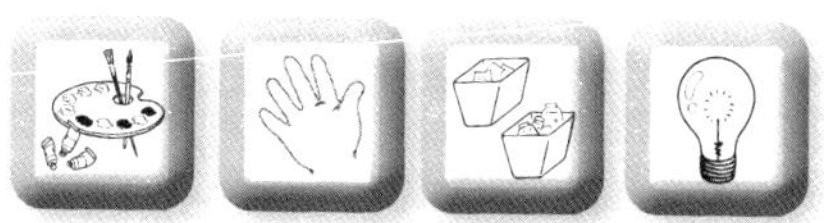

Help children practice fine motor skills by completing Reproducible 5: Connect the Dots on **page 84**.

To help children improve visual discrimination skills, have them complete Reproducible 6: Can You Find 100? on **page 85**. Children must find the five 100s hidden in the picture on the page.

Have children build higher-order thinking skills and fluency by completing Reproducible 7: Match the Number to the Number Word on **page 86**.

My name is: ____ .

Color by Number

Directions: Color by number this picture.

1 – yellow
2 – purple
3 – pink
4 – green
5 – red
6 – peach
7 – brown
8 – blue

Traced Verse

Directions: Trace the verse.

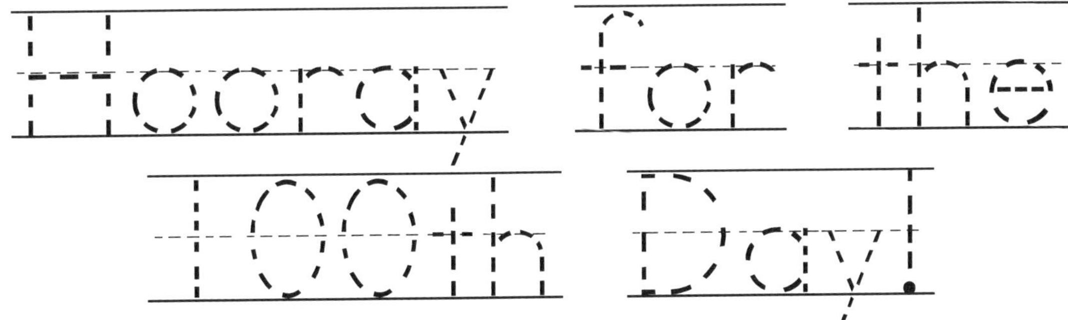

Handwriting Practice

Directions: Now copy the verse on the line below.

____

- -

____

- -

My name is: _______________________________.

I Can Find One (1)

   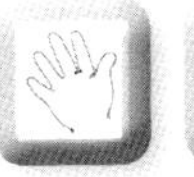 

My name is: _______________________________ .

I Can Find Two (2)

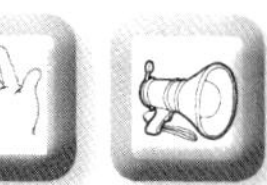

My name is: _________________________ .

I Can Find Three (3)

My name is: _______________________________ .

I Can Find Four (4)

My name is: _________________________ .

I Can Find Five (5)

My name is: _______________________________ .

I Can Find Six (6)

My name is: ___________________________________ .

Directions: Think of five ways in which you have grown and changed in the first 100 days of school. Complete each sentence starter and draw a picture to go with each one.

1. **I try to** ____ .

2. **I am better at** ____ .

3. **I am friends with** ____ .

4. **I learned to** ____ .

5. **I know new words like** _______________________________________ .

My name is: ______________________________________ .

Directions: Read each example aloud and then ask children to respond Yes or No.

Are 100 jelly beans the same as 100 bricks?

Why or why not? ____ .

____

Are 100 cotton balls the same as 100 rubber balls?

Why or why not? ____ .

____

Are 100 __________ the same as 100 __________?

Why or why not? ____ .

____

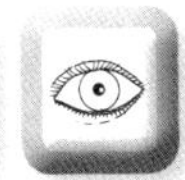

My name is: ______________________________________ .

Directions: Place your pencil on the number 1 and connect the dots in order to make something to help you celebrate. What picture did you make?

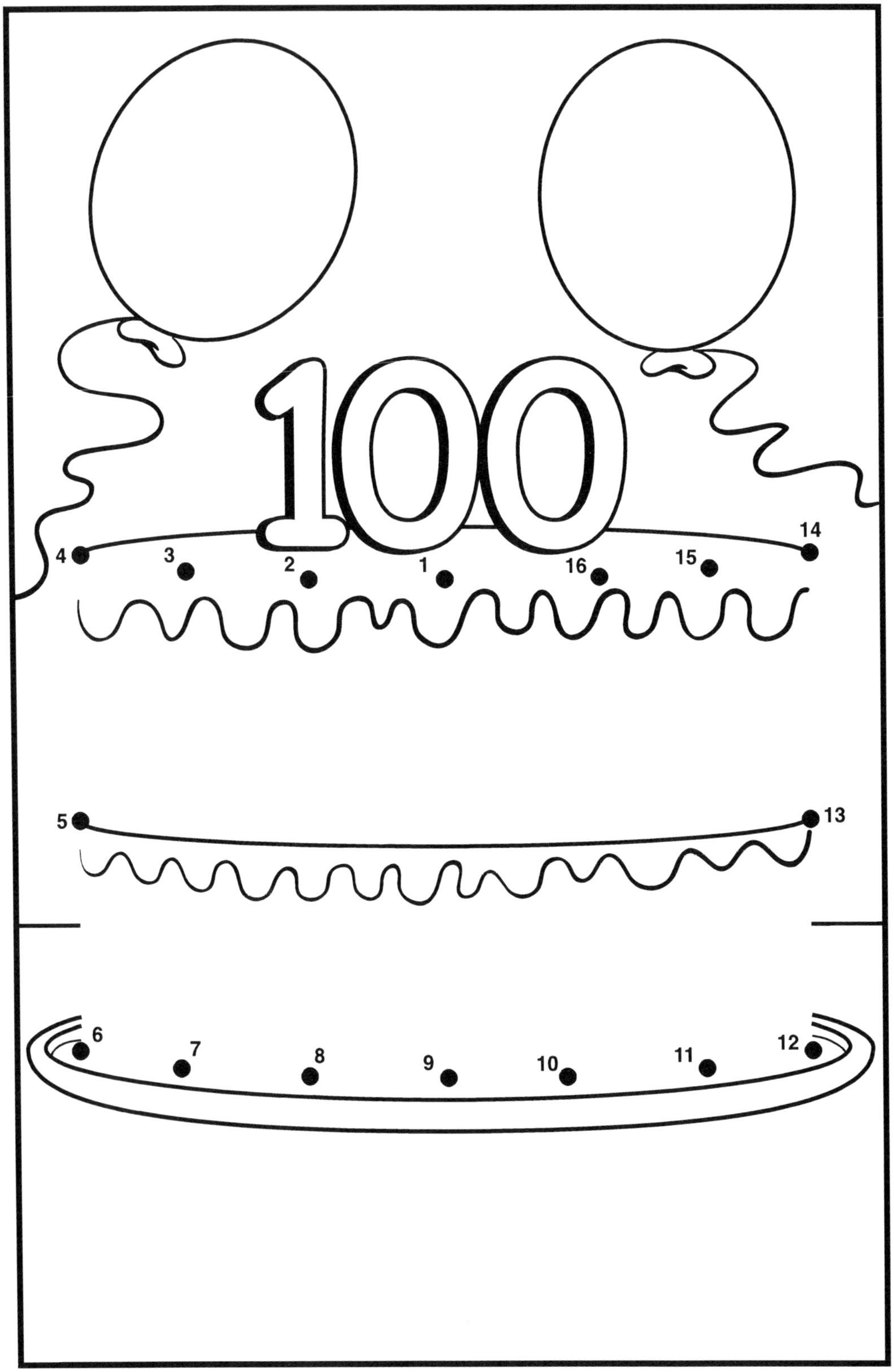

This is a picture of: ____.

Reproducible 6: Can You Find 100?

   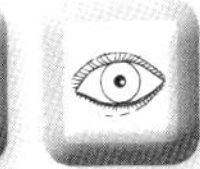

My name is: ________________________________ .

Directions: In the picture below, the number 100 is hiding in five places. Circle the number 100 when you find it. Use a blue crayon.

 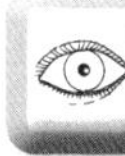   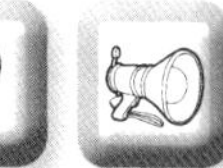

My name is: ___________________________________ .

Directions: Draw a line from the number to the number word that matches it.

1	five
5	one hundred
10	one
100	ten

Chapter Nine

Almost Late Again! The Concept of Time

Almost Late Again!

Hurry, hurry, don't be late.
The clock is ticking and will not wait.
Hours and minutes slipping by,
Quickly time begins to fly.

Get up now and wash your face.
Time to start the daily race.
Eat your pancakes, watch the clock.
The minutes tick while you find your sock.

Look at the hands winking at you.
Covering the numbers . . . 12, 1, 2,
On to 3, 4, 5, 6, 7,
Passing by 8, 9, 10, and 11.

Helping to plan or maybe to worry,
The clock lets us rest or hurry.
Counting out the dark and light,
Twelve hours for day and twelve for night.

Run to the school yard or catch the bus,
Time won't wait for any of us.
Sixty minutes in each hour,
That's the measure of its power.

Twenty four hours in each day,
You can choose to spend it your way.
Busy or quiet, happy or sad,
Make it the best you've ever had!

Brain-Building Activities

The enrichment activities for "Almost Late Again!" on **page 87** are brief since telling time is an abstract concept for young children. The purpose of this poem is to simply acquaint children with the concept of telling time and with some of the terms used in telling time.

After reading "Almost Late Again!" aloud, ask children to count the number of clocks or watches in their homes that evening. The next day, invite children to share the number of clocks or watches with the group. You may want to write down the number of clocks and watches and graph the numbers using cubes or blocks to show the comparison.

Children begin to build confidence about the words that go with time concepts with Reproducible 1: Color by Number, Traced Verse, and Handwriting Practice on **page 89**.

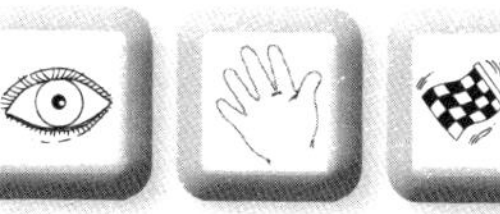

You can use Reproducible 2: Pattern of a Clock Face with Hands to Cut Out on **page 90** to help children practice telling time by the hour. Help them cut out and attach the hour and minute hands using a metal brad.

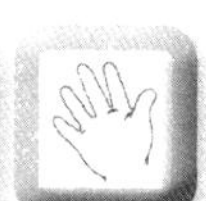

Discuss the concept of using time wisely. This is an abstract concept linked to emotional and social intelligence. Ask, "Even though we cannot see time, can we still lose it or waste it?" Give examples to help the children build schema. Reproducible 3: Transparency: Wise Use of Time on **page 91** to organize the students' responses.

Children can practice using "time words" by completing Reproducible 4: When Is a Good Time? on **page 92**.

Introduce the term *o'clock* and explain how the hands on the clock point to the hour.

Help children understand the problems that may arise when time is not watched carefully. Reproducible 5: Cause and Effect on **page 93** will allow children to practice cause-and-effect critical thinking by drawing a circle around each event that might be caused by a time issue.

Many important words and concepts are associated with telling time. Use Reproducible 6: Finding the Time on **page 94** circle the items that can tell us the time.

Using Reproducible 7: Listening for CK and CH on **page 95** to build auditory discrimination for the phonemes CH and CK found in the words CLOCK and WATCH.

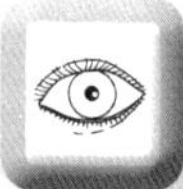

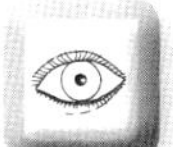

My name is: _______________________________________ .

Color by Number

Directions: Color by number this picture.

1 – brown
2 – light blue
3 – yellow
4 – dark green
5 – light green

Traced Verse

Directions: Trace the verse.

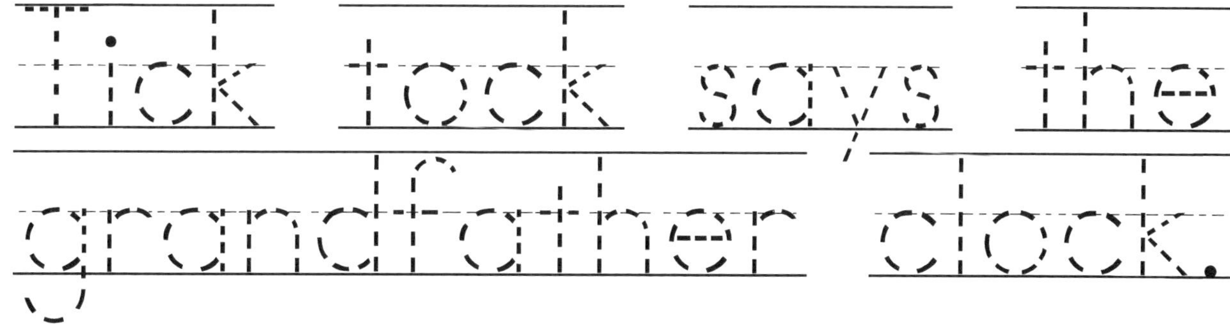

Handwriting Practice

Directions: Now copy the verse on the line below.

____

____

Directions: Cut out the clock face and hands. Your teacher will help you to fasten the two hands of the clock with brads so the hands move.

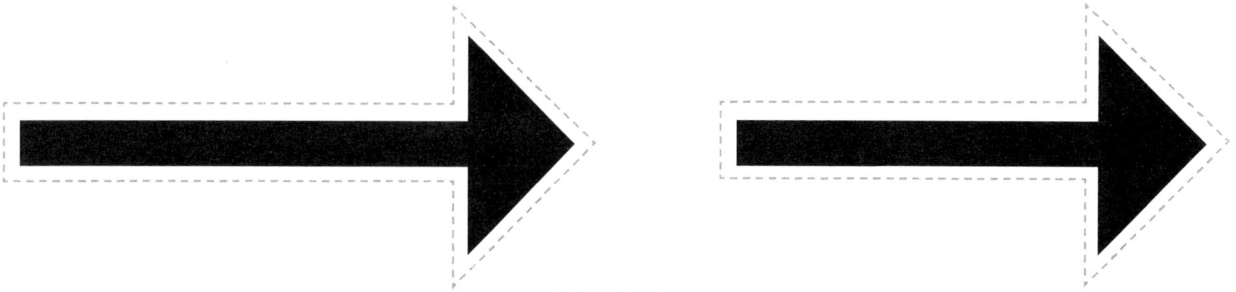

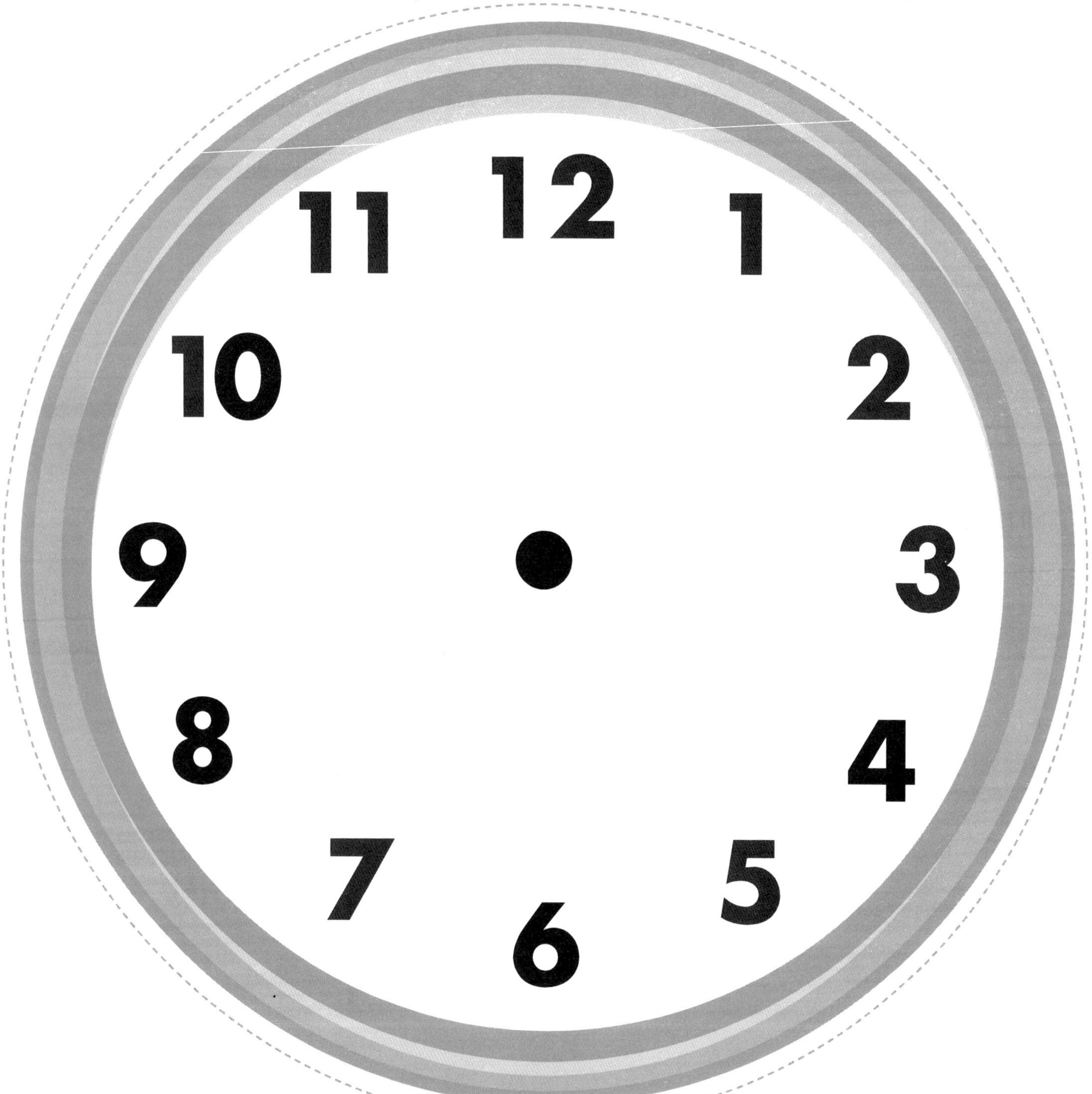

Directions: Use this page as a transparency on which to record the students' responses to the question, "How can I use the gift of time wisely?"

How Can I Use the Gift of Time Wisely?

At Home

With Friends

At Play

Quiet Times

At School

My name is: _________________________________ .

Directions: Look at each picture. Think of a good time to do each thing in each picture.

_______________ o'clock is a good time for this.

_______________ o'clock is a good time for this.

_______________ o'clock is a good time for this.

My name is: ____ .

Directions: In each row, there is a picture that shows what can happen when we are not thinking about time. Circle the picture with your crayon.

1	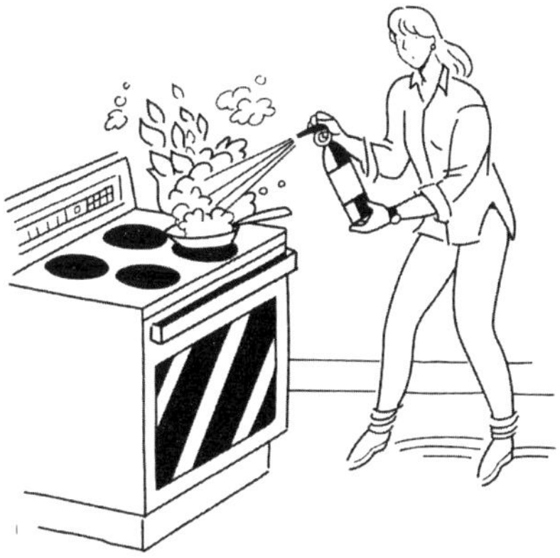	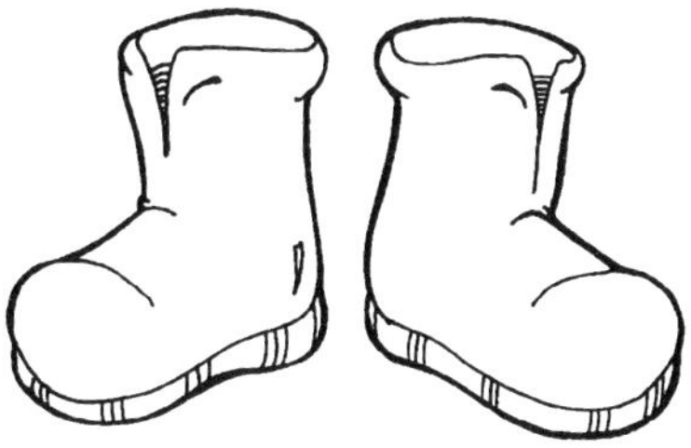
2	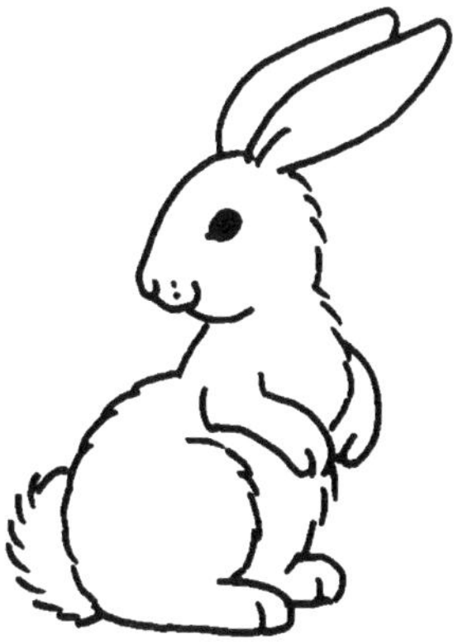	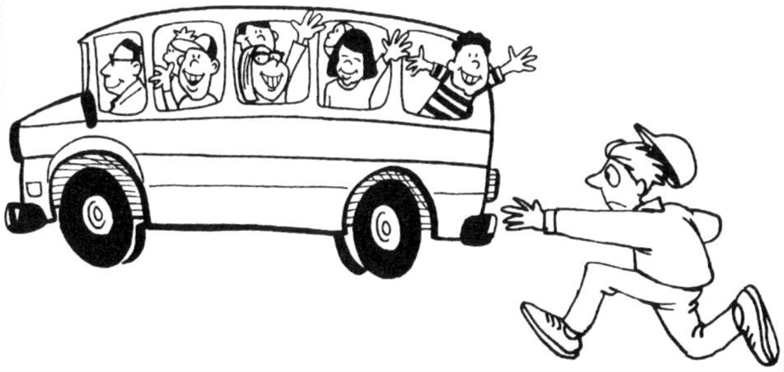
3	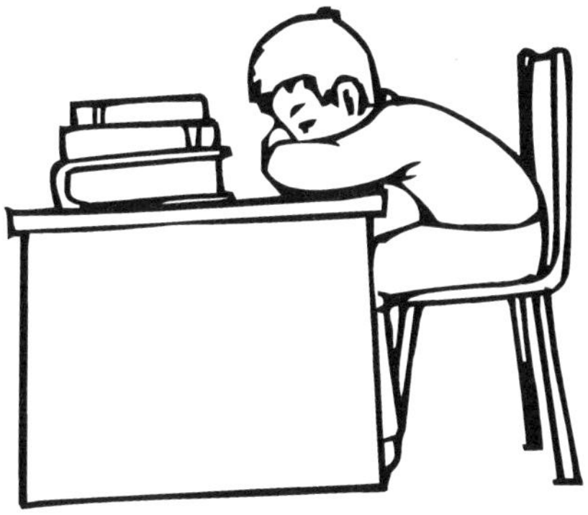	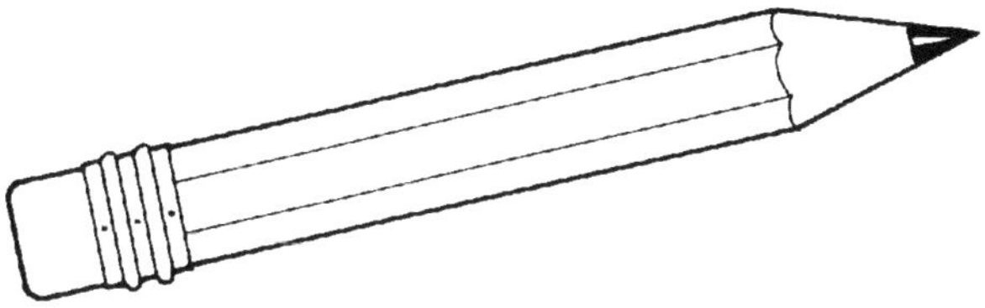
4	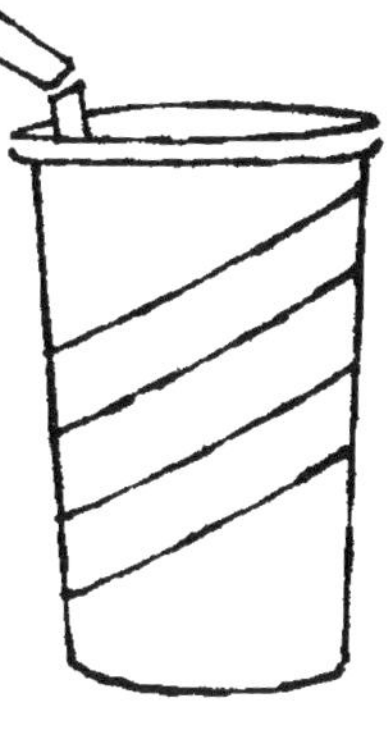	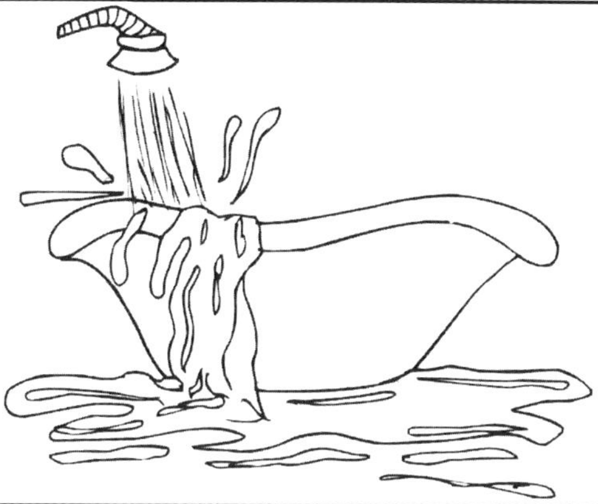

Reproducible 6: Finding the Time

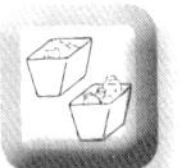

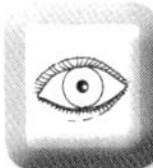

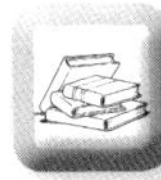

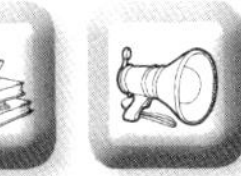

My name is: ________________________________ .

Directions: Circle the items that can tell us the time. There will be four that belong and two that do not belong.

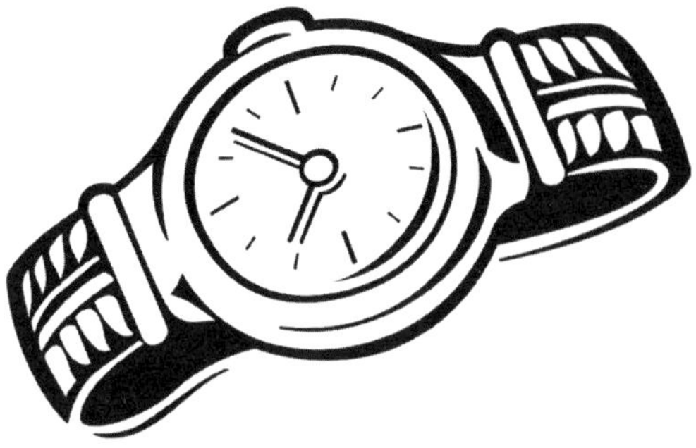

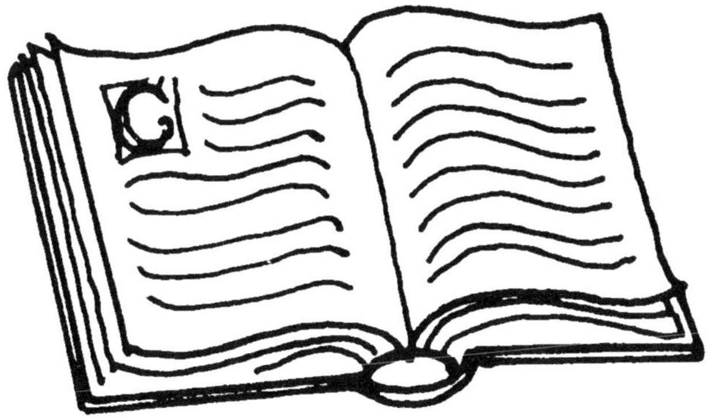

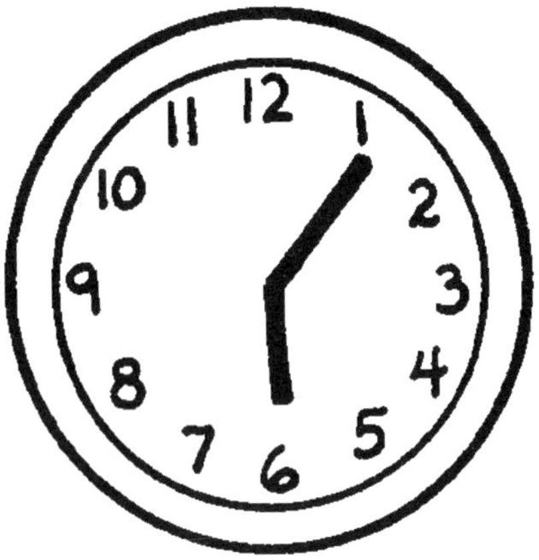

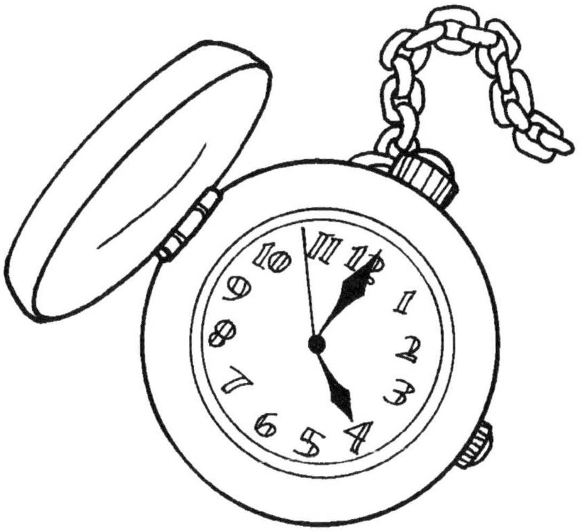

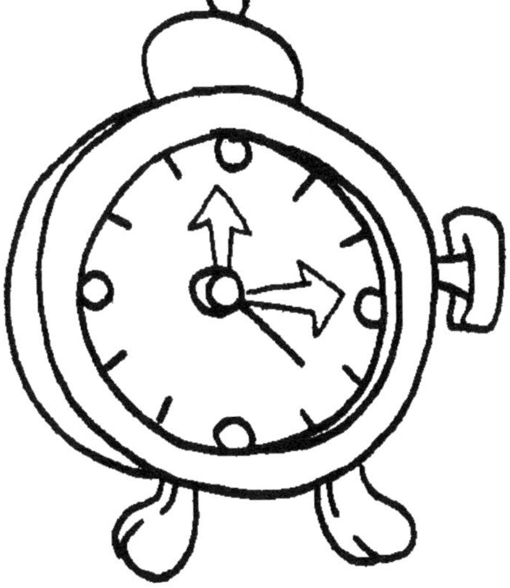

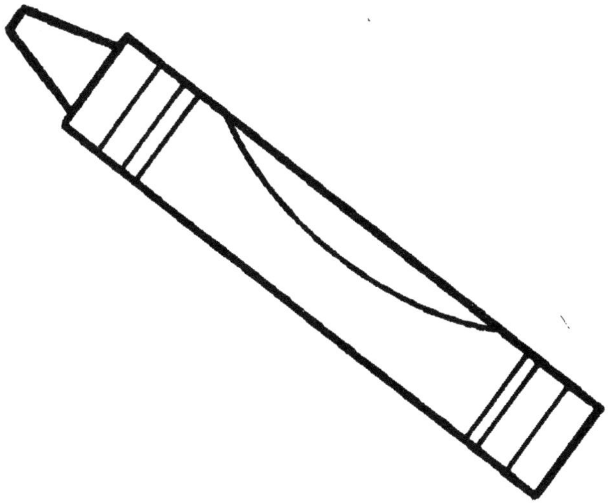

My name is: _______________________________ .

Directions: There are six pictures below. Listen as your teacher says the word that matches each picture. Write **CK** or **CH** on the line to match the **ending sound** of each word.

_______________ _______________ _______________

 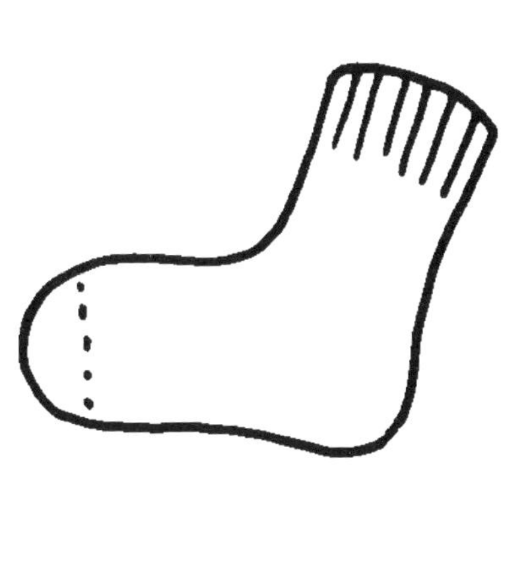 

_______________ _______________ _______________

Chapter Ten
Thankfully Yours:
Thinking About Reasons to Be Thankful

Directions: Use this poem as the insert for a Thanksgiving card children can decorate and take home.

Thankfully Yours

I'm thankful for the harvest,
The gifts of corn and wheat,
For rows of orange pumpkins,
and apples crisp and sweet.

I'm thankful for the seasons,
The stars and moon and sun.
Yes, there are many reasons,
It's hard to name just one.

I'm thankful for those who love me
And take the time to care,
Especially my family,
Because they are always there.

I'm thankful for the food we eat,
The turkey and stuffing and bread,
And don't forget something sweet
After thanks has been said.

I'm thankful to be living here
In a country proud and free.
Thanksgiving time is drawing near,
And I'm thankful to be me.

Brain-Building Activities

After reading the poem "Thankfully Yours" on **page 96** aloud, invite children to learn stanzas as a choral reading and present it to parents during a harvest-time PTA meeting or a community performance.

Use Reproducible 1: Color by Number, Traced Verse, and Handwriting Practice on **page 99** to develop fine motor and visual discrimination. The children can trace the verse, and then, on the bottom line, copy the verse.

Reproducible 2: Rebus Story on **page 100** is a good way to build reading skills and visual discrimination.

Use chart paper and scented makers to make a list of things, people, and opportunities for which the children are thankful. After writing the children's responses, ask, "Is it good or bad that every person is thankful for different things?"

Make a "Thankful For" page for each student in your class. Give each child a copy of Reproducible 3: Thankfully Thinking and Doing on **page 101**. Ask the children to cut out pictures from magazines that represent things for which they are thankful and glue them to the page.

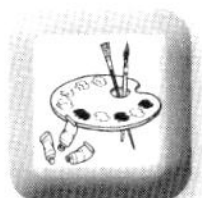

Create a Thanksgiving card to send home to each family by using Reproducible 4: Thanksgiving Card on **page 102**.

Use Reproducible 5: Amazing Harvest Maze on **page 103** to practice fine motor and visual discrimination skills.

Children can practice counting and ordering skills by completing Reproducible 6: Connect the Dots on **page 104**.

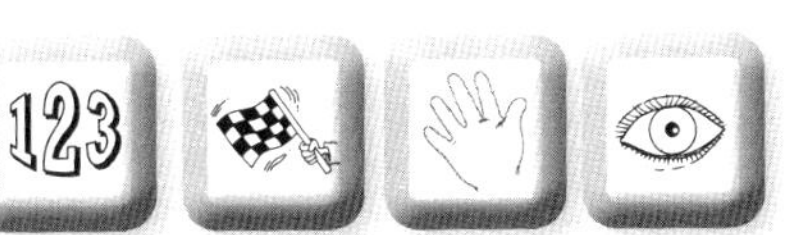

Use paper cups of candy corn or unpopped popcorn as manipulatives to solve the simple addition and subtraction problems found Reproducible 7: Math Harvest on **page 105**.

Comparing *same* and *different* is an important early childhood skill. Using Reproducible 8: Same and Different on **page 106**, children are to circle the item that does not belong.

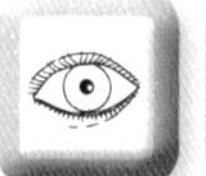

Ordering from largest to smallest is a critical thinking skill. Have children use Reproducible 9: Largest to Smallest on **page 107** to cut out harvest vegetables and order them from largest to smallest.

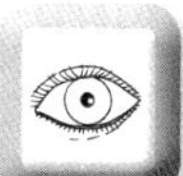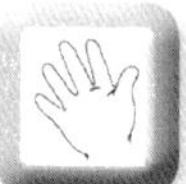

Bring in examples of interesting autumn vegetables such as gourds, corn, pumpkins, and winter squash. Give children an opportunity to touch, smell, and weigh each item using a kitchen scale.

Cut some smaller squash pieces or gourds in half and use them for "veggie patch painting." Dip the pieces, flat side down, into poster or tempera paint and let the children create veggie pictures by pressing them onto white paper.

Take each child's picture with a digital camera and then mount it onto the pumpkin cut-out found on Reproducible 10: Pumpkin Cut-Out on **page 108**. Create a display in your classroom titled "A Harvest of Beautiful Children."

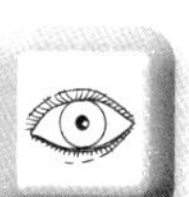

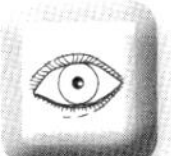    

My name is: ___________________________________ .

Color by Number

Directions: Color by number this picture.

1 – orange
2 – yellow
3 – brown
4 – greem
5 – red
6 – purple
7 – light blue
8 – dark blue

Traced Verse

Directions: Trace the verse.

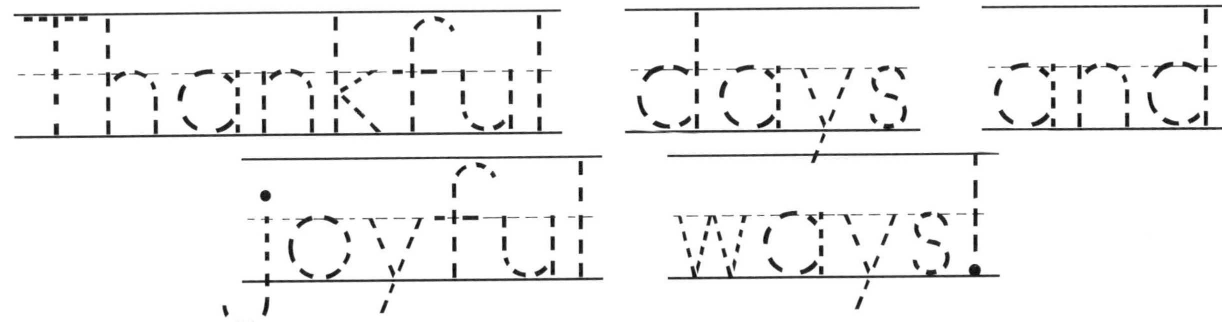

Handwriting Practice

Directions: Now copy the verse on the line below.

My name is: ________________________________ .

Directions: Cut out the picture boxes at the bottom of the page. Paste the pictures into the story where they belong. Read your story to a friend.

I want to say "thank you" for my  . They love

me. I want to say "thank you" for the  that we

eat. I want to say "thank you" for the  in the

sky. I want to say "thank you" for my  where I

can learn to read this story!

My name is: _________________________________ .

Directions: Cut out magazine pictures and glue them in the space below to show things for which you are thankful.

_________________________________'s Page of Thanks

Handmade by

   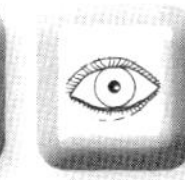

My name is: ___________________________________ .

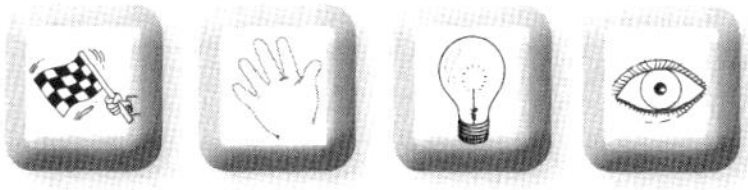

Directions: Place your pencil on the dot that says *begin,* and find the shortest, clear path to the Amazing Harvest Market where fruits and vegetables wait for you to take them home.

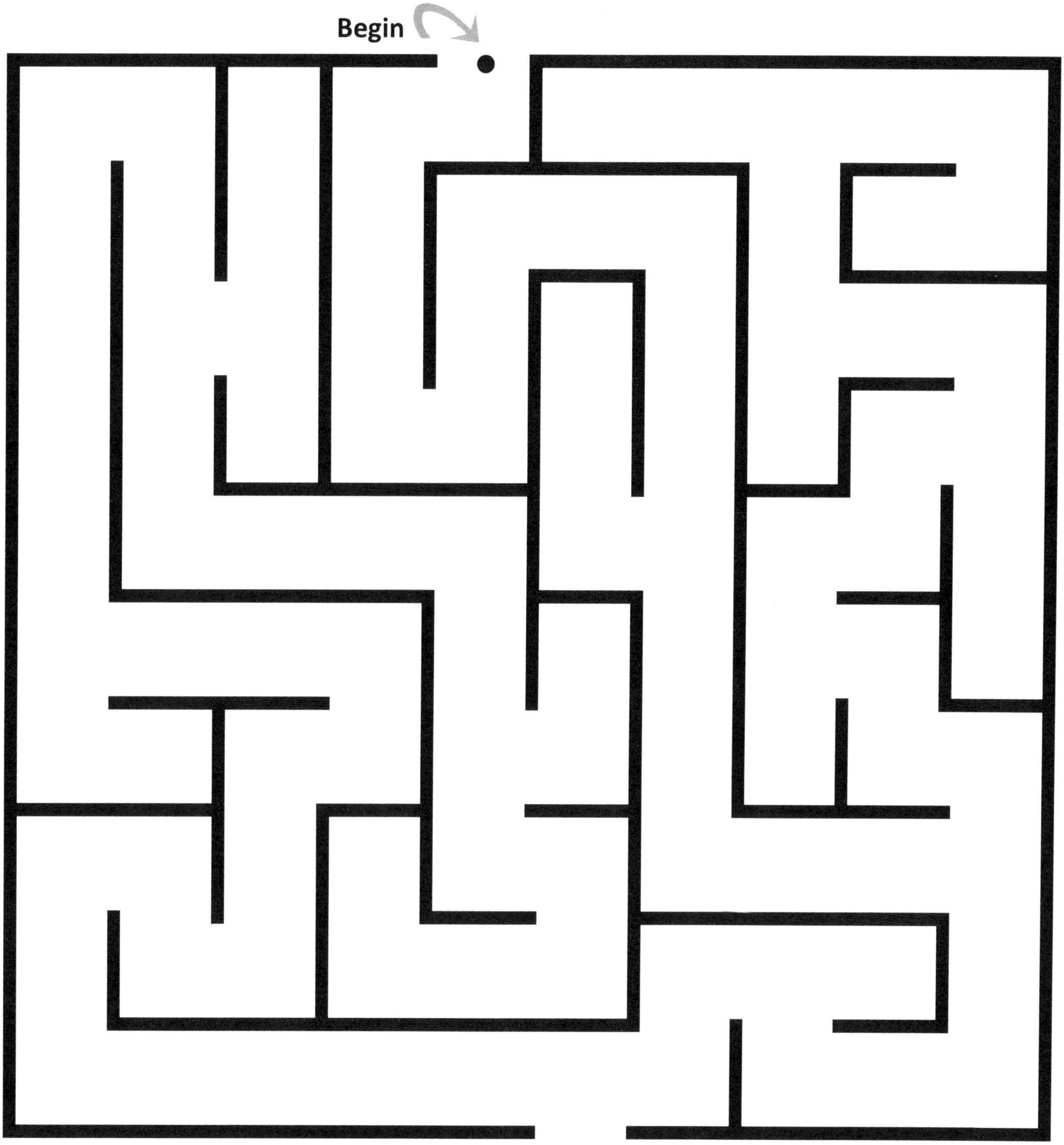

Begin

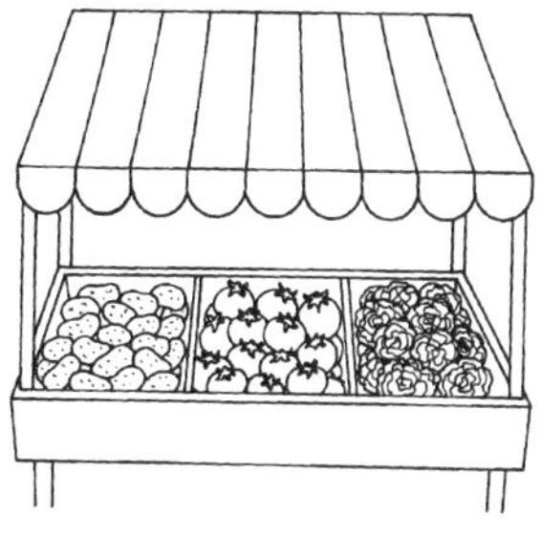

   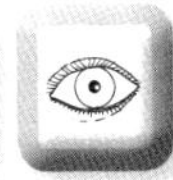

My name is: ____ .

Directions: Place your pencil on the number 1 and connect the dots in order. What harvest vegetable did you make?

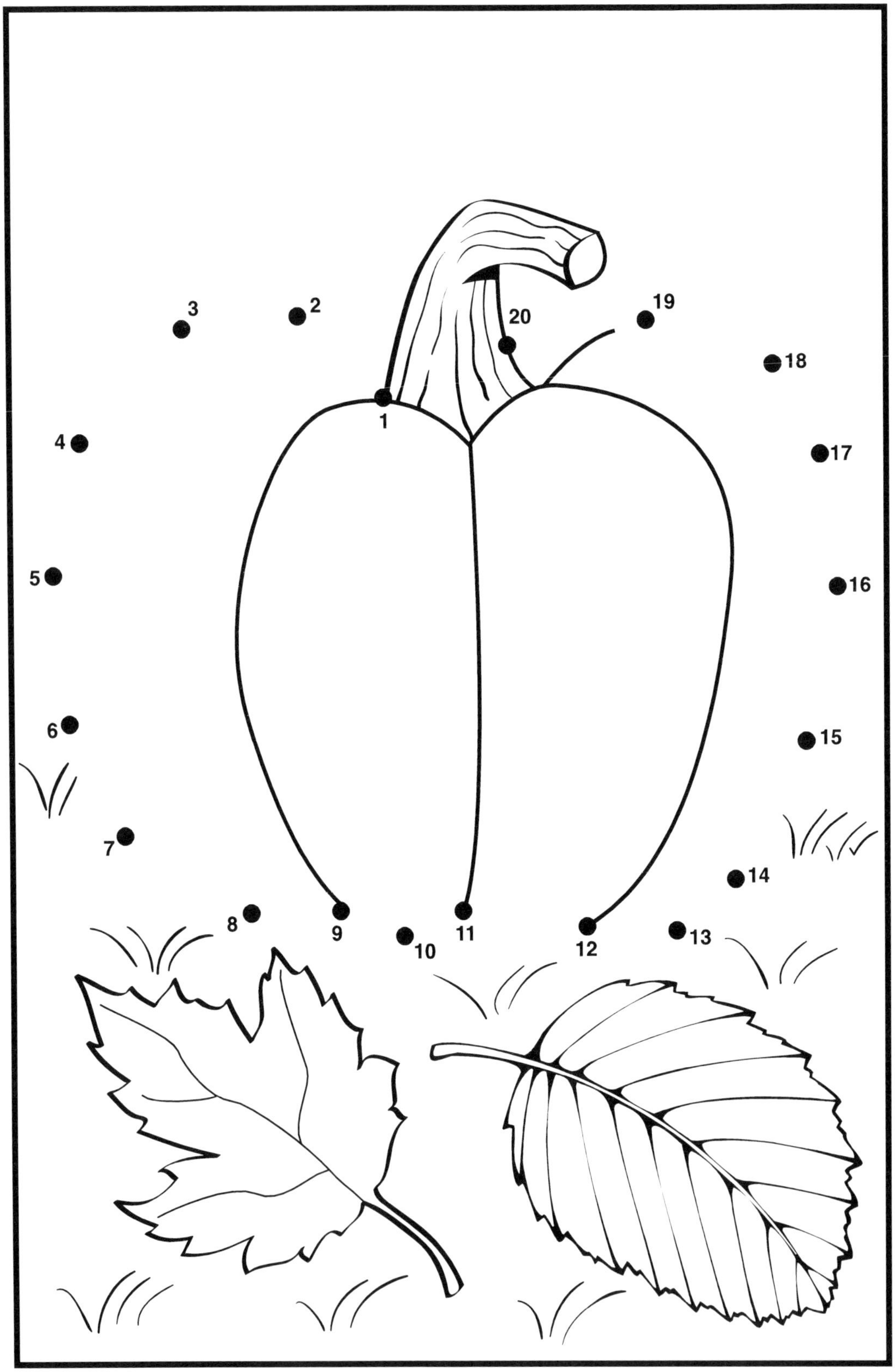

This is a picture of: ____ .

  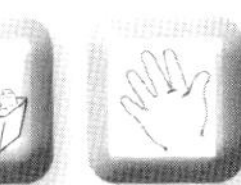

My name is: _______________________________________ .

Directions: Use your cup of corn counters to solve the problems below. If you are using candy corn, you may eat your solution to each problem! If you are using unpopped popcorn, you may glue your solution into each box. On each ear of corn, color in the right number of kernels to show your answer, too.

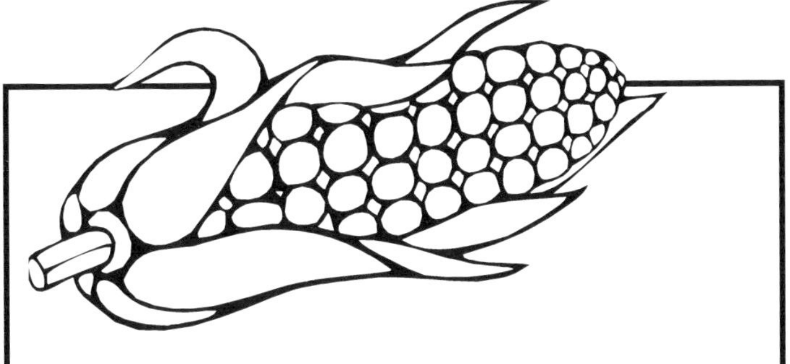

6 + 2 = _________

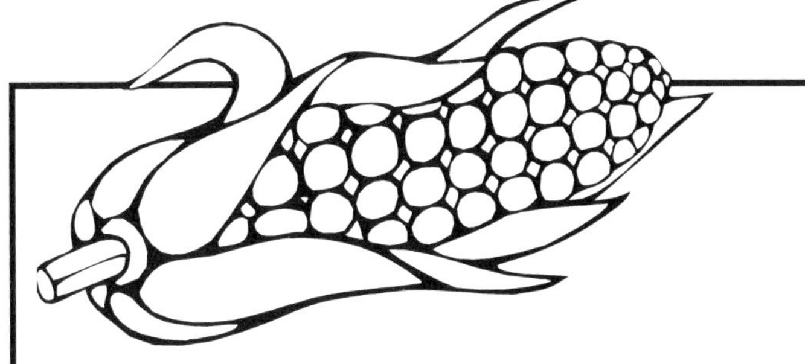

5 − 2 = _________

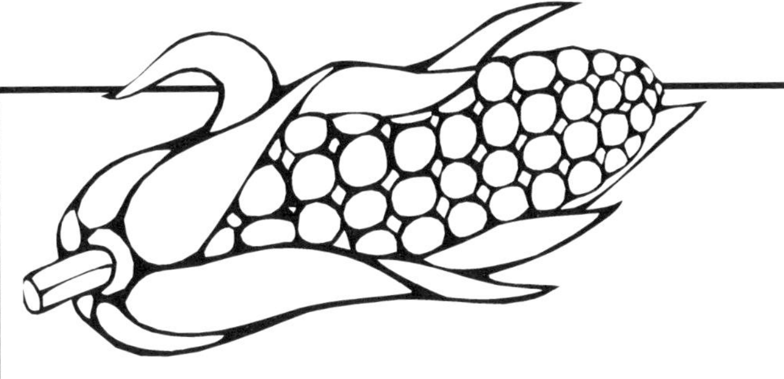

4 − 1 = _________

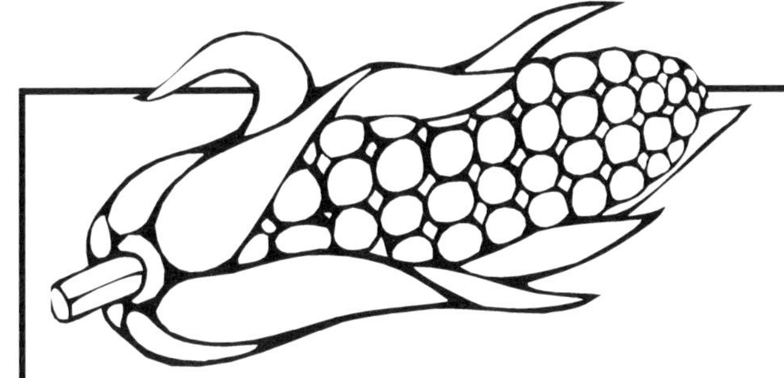

3 + 3 = _________

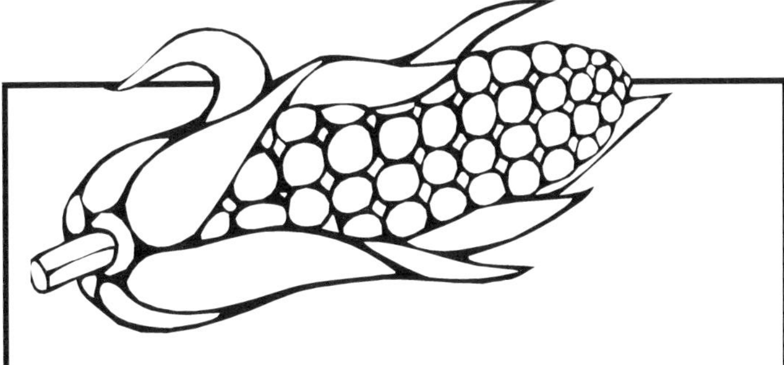

2 + 1 = _________

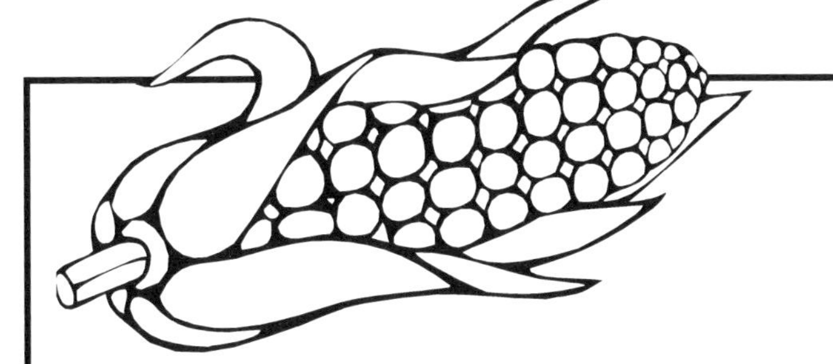

4 + 0 = _________

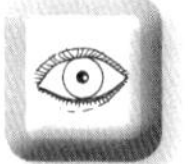 

My name is: ________________________________ .

Directions: In each row, circle the item that does not belong in the same group.

1			
2			
3			
4			
5			
6			
7			

 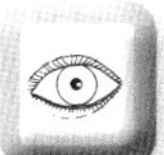  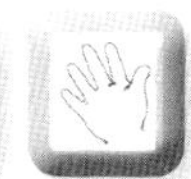

My name is: ________________________________ .

Directions: Cut out the pictures at the bottom of the page. Glue them in order from largest to smallest in the boxes below.

Pumpkins

1.   2.   3.

Squirrels

1.   2.   3.

Leaves

1.   2.   3.

 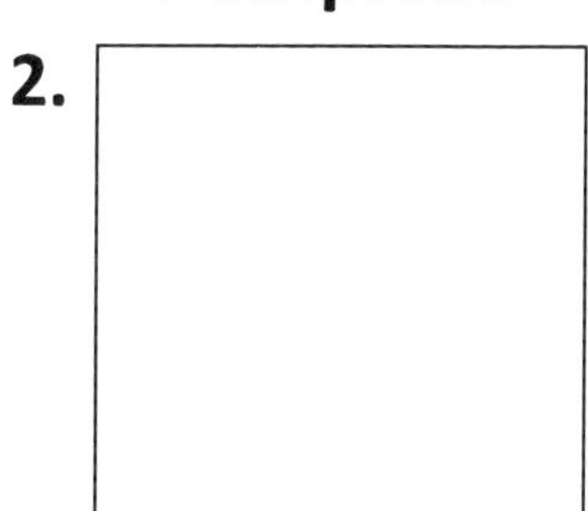 

 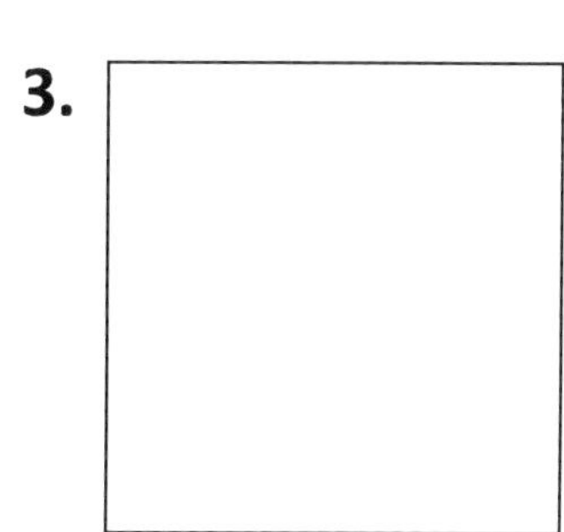

 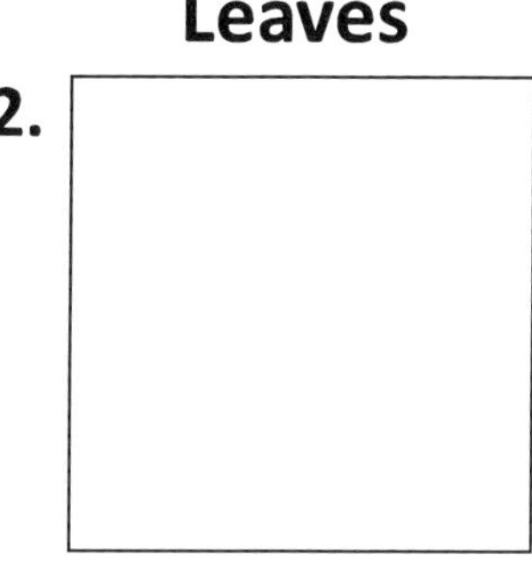 

Reproducible 10: Pumpkin Cut-Out

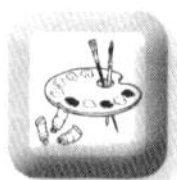

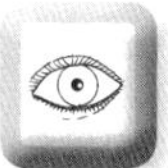

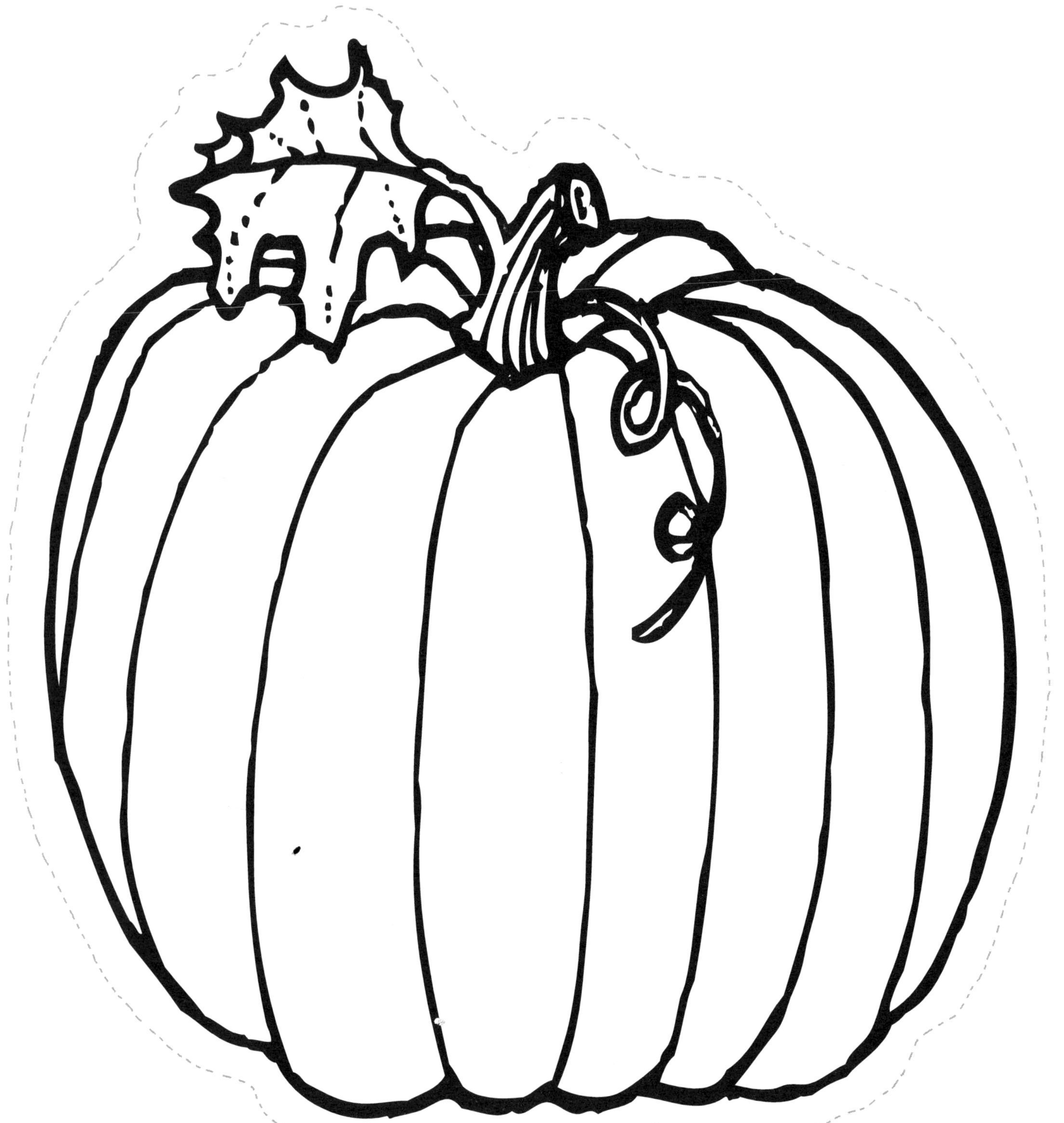

Chapter Eleven

Mind Your Manners: Positive Polite Behavior Connects People and Brain Cells

Mind Your Manners

Please and thank you, thank you please,
Minding manners with words like these.
Showing courtesy every day,
At home and school, at work and play.

Never shoving, thank you please.
Minding manners with choices like these.
Acting with courtesy every day,
At home and school, at work and play.

Asking nicely, thank you please,
Using manners with tones like these.
Showing courtesy every day,
At home and school, at work and play.

Sharing snacks, thank you please,
Showing kindness with choices like these.
Acting with courtesy every day,
At home and school, at work and play.

Walking quietly, thank you please,
Being respectful with steps like these.
Showing courtesy every day,
At home and school, at work and play.

Politeness to the teacher, thank you please,
Minding your manners with words like these.
Living your courtesy every day,
At home and school, at work and play.

Brain-Building Activities

After reading "Mind Your Manners" on **page 109**, ask children to respond to the following questions:

- What is courtesy? Is it hard to be courteous, or is it simple?
- How can you show politeness to your teacher?
- What is respect? Can you name some people you respect?
- Why is it important to talk quietly at school?
- Should you use manners at home and at school?
- Name some other places where using good manners are important.

Using chart paper or an interactive whiteboard, create a list of the children's expressive language responses. Put each child's name next to his or her response to connect the auditory and visual modalities. Example: *Katie says, "I wait in line nicely at lunch."*

"Mind Your Manners" on **page 109** is a nice vehicle for using hand puppets to role-play ordinary classroom behaviors or scenarios. Use real world events to allow children to use constructivism to create their own knowledge.

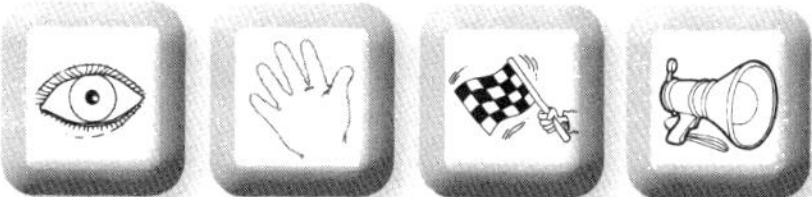

Use Reproducible 1: Color by Number, Traced Verse, and Handwriting Practice on **page 111** to develop fine motor and visual discrimination. The children can trace the verse, and then, on the bottom line, copy the verse.

Create a "Courtesy Counts" booklet by having children illustrate each of the four mini-pages on Reproducible 2: Courtesy Counts Mini-Booklet on **page 112**. The pages can be cut out and made into a booklet. Discuss each of the courteous decisions a child can make and how they affect others.

Using Reproducible 3: Rebus Story on **page 113** is a good way for children to build reading skills and visual discrimination.

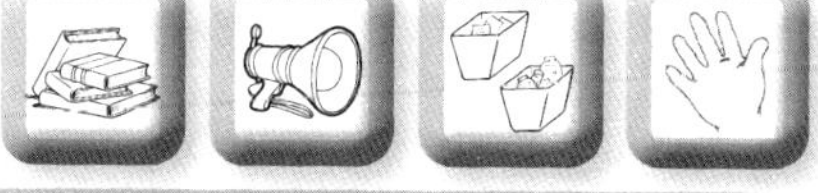

Children can use Reproducible 4: Connect the Dots on **page 114** to practice counting and sequencing skills.

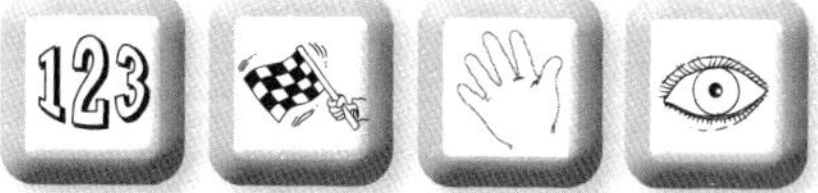

Have children use Reproducible 5: Mind Your Manners Maze on **page 115** to practice fine motor skills.

Establish a system to identify, encourage, and reward acts of good manners and great attitudes in your classroom with a Courtesy Counts estimating jar. Rinse out a quart jar, get some pretty marbles or decorative stones from the craft store, and create a system in which the children (1) can be rewarded by you or another teacher, or (2) can give rewards to one another for acts of courtesy. The recipient gets to put a marble or stone in the jar; when the jar is full or reaches a designated point, the class earns a reward. This can be a tangible reward like a popcorn party or an activity-based award, like extra recess time. Write your target behaviors on Reproducible 6: Courtesy Counts Estimating Jar on **page 116**.

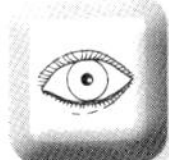    

My name is: ____ .

Color by Number

Directions: Color by number this picture.

1 – brown
2 – dark blue
3 – yellow
4 – green
5 – pink
6 – red
7 – purple
8 – peach
9 – light blue
10 – orange

Traced Verse

Directions: Trace the verse.

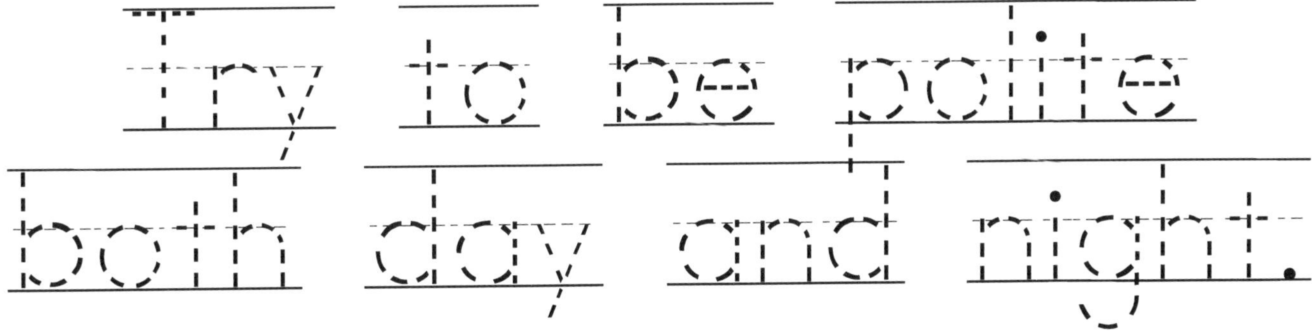

Handwriting Practice

Directions: Now copy the verse on the line below.

My name is: ________________________________ .

Directions: On each of the four mini-pages below you will see a sentence about being courteous. Draw a picture that goes with each sentence. Cut out the pages and make a mini-booklet to remind you about being courteous.

<table>
<tr><td>

Be polite to others.

</td><td>

Let others go first.

</td></tr>
<tr><td>

Let's share our materials.

</td><td>

Say "please" and "thank you."

</td></tr>
</table>

   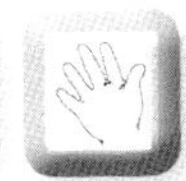

My name is: ____ .

Directions: Cut out the picture boxes at the bottom of the page. Paste the pictures into the story where they belong. Read your story to a friend.

My Story

I use good manners at  . I like to be polite to my

 . I like to do nice things for my friends. Using

good manners makes my  and my 

feel good!

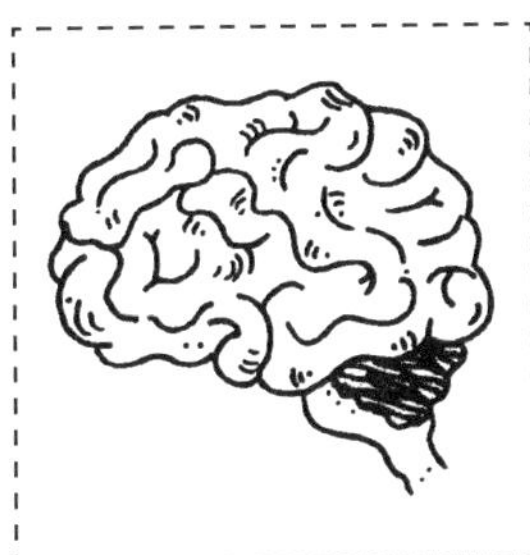   

   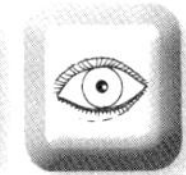

My name is: _______________________________ .

Directions: Place your pencil on the number 1 and connect the dots in order. Do this for each set of dots. What important word did you make?

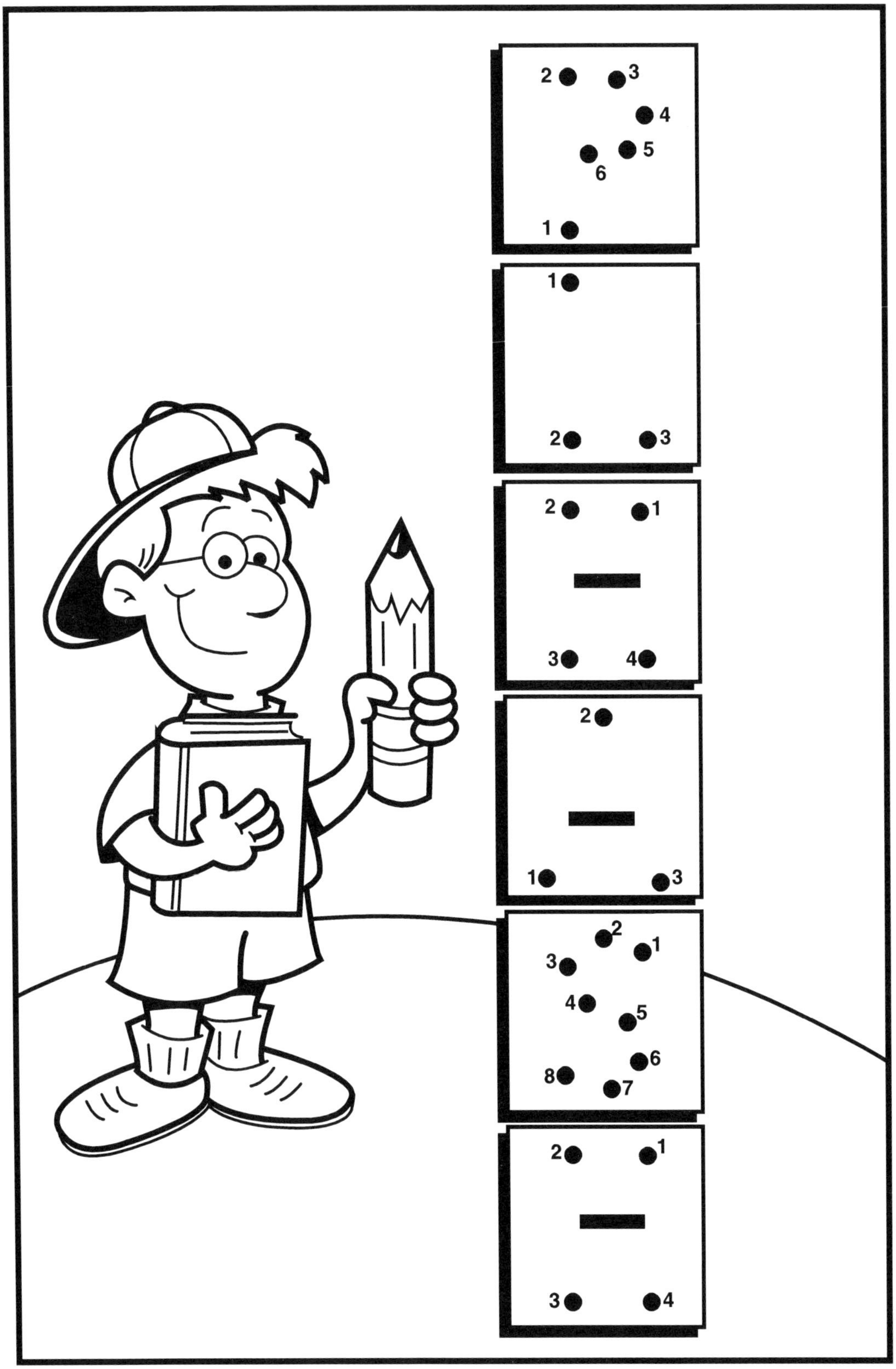

This is a picture of the word _______________________________________.

Reproducible 5: Mind Your Manners Maze

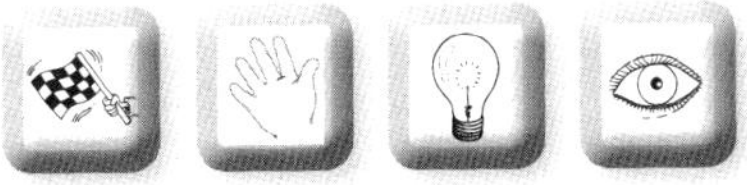

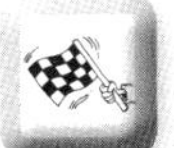

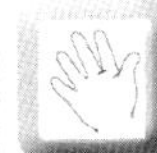

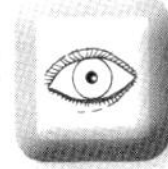

My name is: ______________________________ .

Directions: Put your pencil on the dot that says "begin," and find the shortest, clear path to the sign that says "Mind Your Manners."

Begin

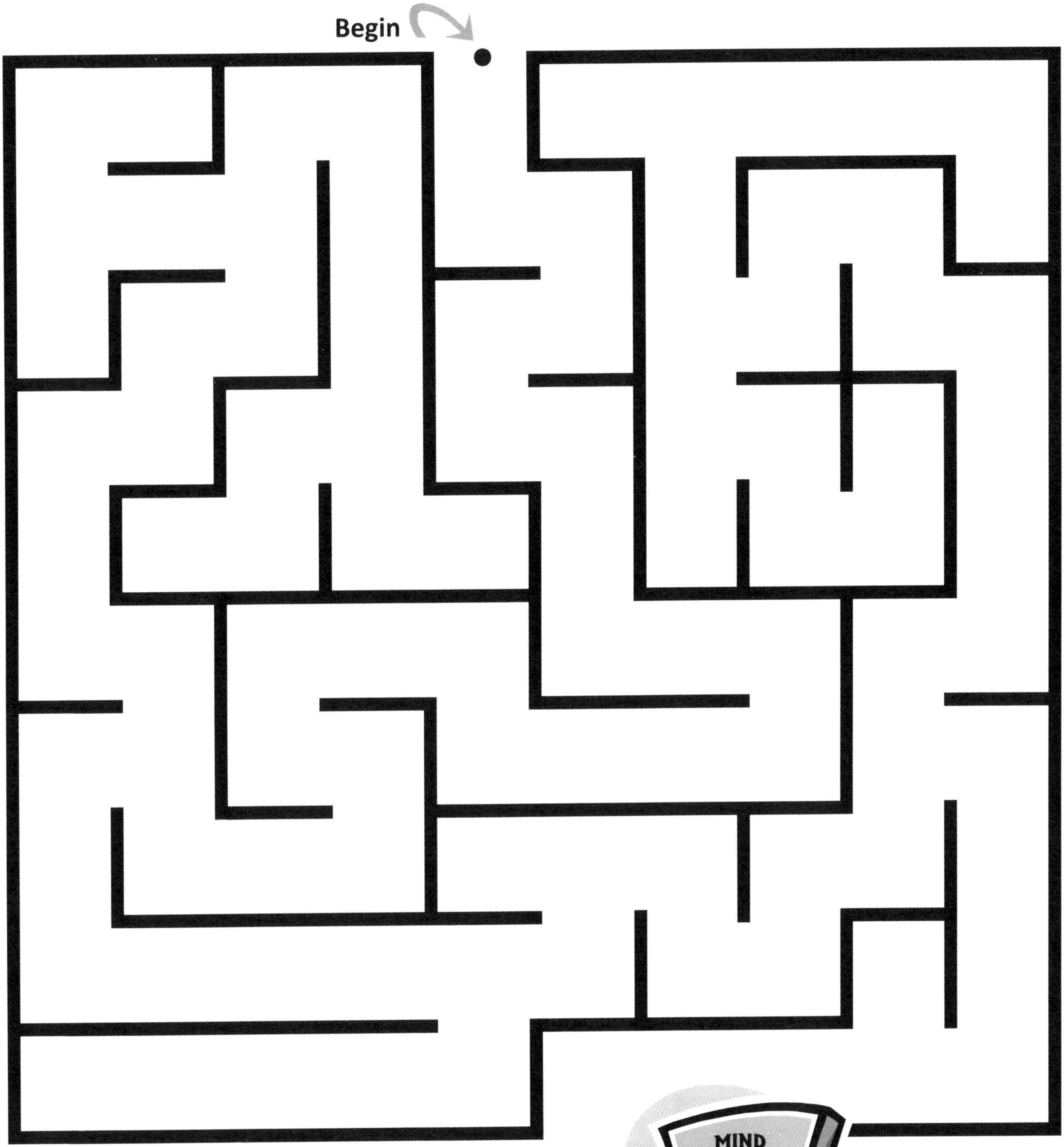

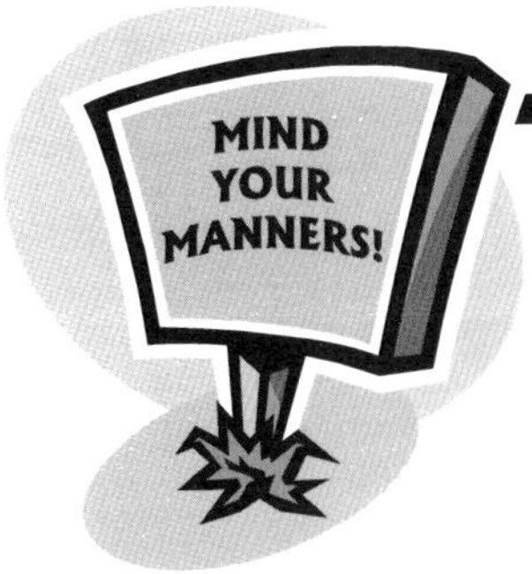

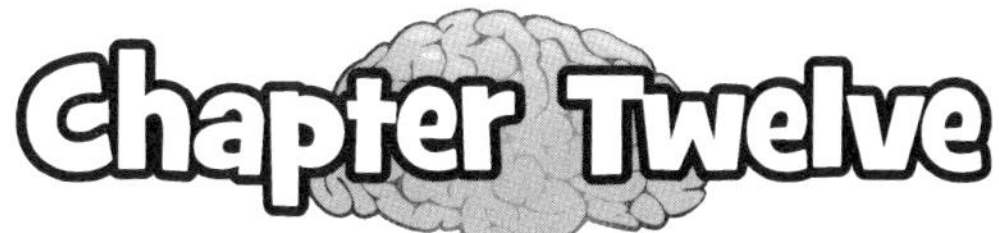

Chapter Twelve

Each Brain Is Unique:
A Celebration of Multiple Intelligences and Classroom Diversity

Each Brain Is Unique

I have a brain and body and mind.
None other like me will you find.
My eyes and hair are one of a kind.
None other like me will you find.

I have a brain and body and mind.
None other like me will you find.
My smile and spirit are one of a kind.
None other like me will you find.

I have a brain and body and mind.
None other like me will you find.
My family and friends are one of a kind.
None other like us will you find.

I have a brain and body and mind.
None other like me will you find.
My skin tone and style are one of a kind.
None other like me will you find.

I have a brain and body and mind.
None other like me will you find.
My thinking and doing are one of a kind.
None other like me will you find.

Unique and special, yet something the same.
We all share the human name.
With brain and body, spirit and soul,
All together, a beautiful whole.

Brain-Building Activities

After reading "Each Brain Is Unique" on **page 117** aloud, write the words *different, diversity,* and *unique* on the board. Discuss the meanings of each word, and use each in a sentence. Give children the opportunity to use the words. Then ask the following questions:

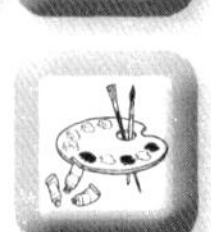

- Do you think every person looks the same, or is every person different?
- Is it a good thing for each person to be different or unique?
- What are some ways we are the same?
- What are some ways we are different?
- Do you like having lots of different friends at school?

Using large sheets of butcher paper, guide children in tracing life-sized outlines of themselves. Over the course of the unit, add in "parts" such as eyes, hair, and clothing as you build schema or concepts about differences and unique attributes of self.

This is a good time to introduce the globe and map of the world. Explain the concept of a large world with many different countries in which children live. Show children North America and help them to say the words correctly.

- "We live in _______________________." [the United States or Canada]
- "We live in the state or province of _______________________."
- "We live in the town or city of _______________________."

Write these phrases on the board or on chart paper so children can associate your expressive and written language.

Bring in illustrated books from the library that show children living in different countries and cultures. Leave the books in a basket in the reading center next to a globe. Give children time to look through these books.

Show children a model or picture of the brain. Explain that every person's brain is unique and different and that there are different ways to be smart. The Multiple Intelligences Assessment: Different Ways to Be Smart on **page 6** in Chapter One may be useful here.

- Some children like to use words.
- Some children like to use music.
- Some children like to draw and paint.
- Some children like to dance and move.
- Some children like to plan and do things.
- Some children like to be outside in nature.
- Some children like to use numbers and shapes.
- Some children like to think and help others.

Use Reproducible 1: Color by Number, Traced Verse, and Handwriting Practice on **page 120** to develop fine motor and visual discrimination. The children can trace the verse, and then, on the bottom line, copy the verse.

Reproducible 2: Rebus Story on **page 121** is a good way to build reading skills and visual discrimination.

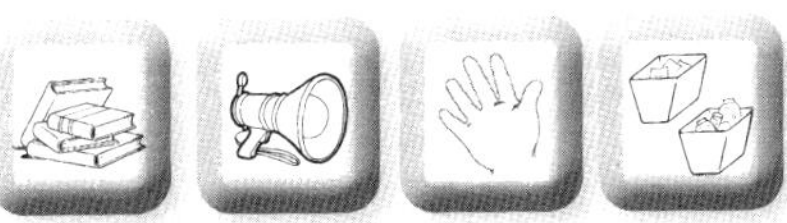

Children can complete Reproducible 3: Connect the Dots on **page 122** to practice counting and sequencing skills.

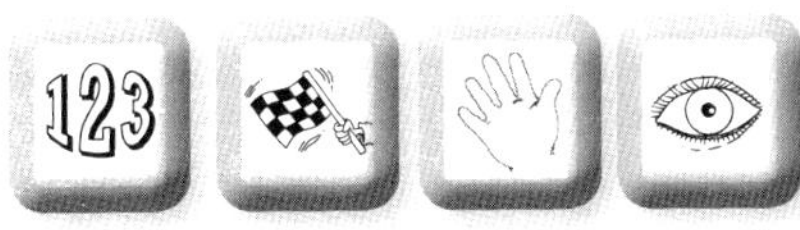

Have children use Reproducible 4: Making Friends Maze on **page 123** to practice fine motor skills.

Practice counting skills with Reproducible 5: Counting with Colors on **page 124**. Children use paper cups of colorful puffed or circle cereal to serve as counting manipulatives.

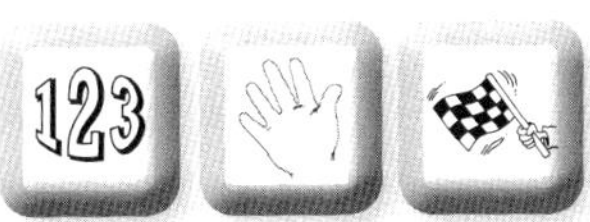

Help children identify and appreciate their unique appearance with Reproducible 6: I Am Special Booklet on **page 125**. It guides children in creating stories about themselves.

Develop critical thinking skills with Reproducible 7: Which One Doesn't Belong? on **page 126**.

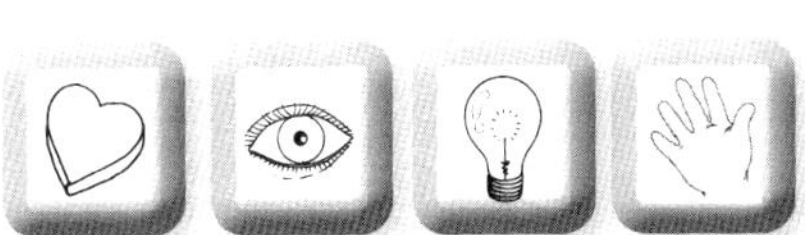

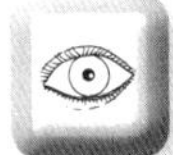

My name is: _______________________________________ .

Color by Number

Directions: Color by number this picture.

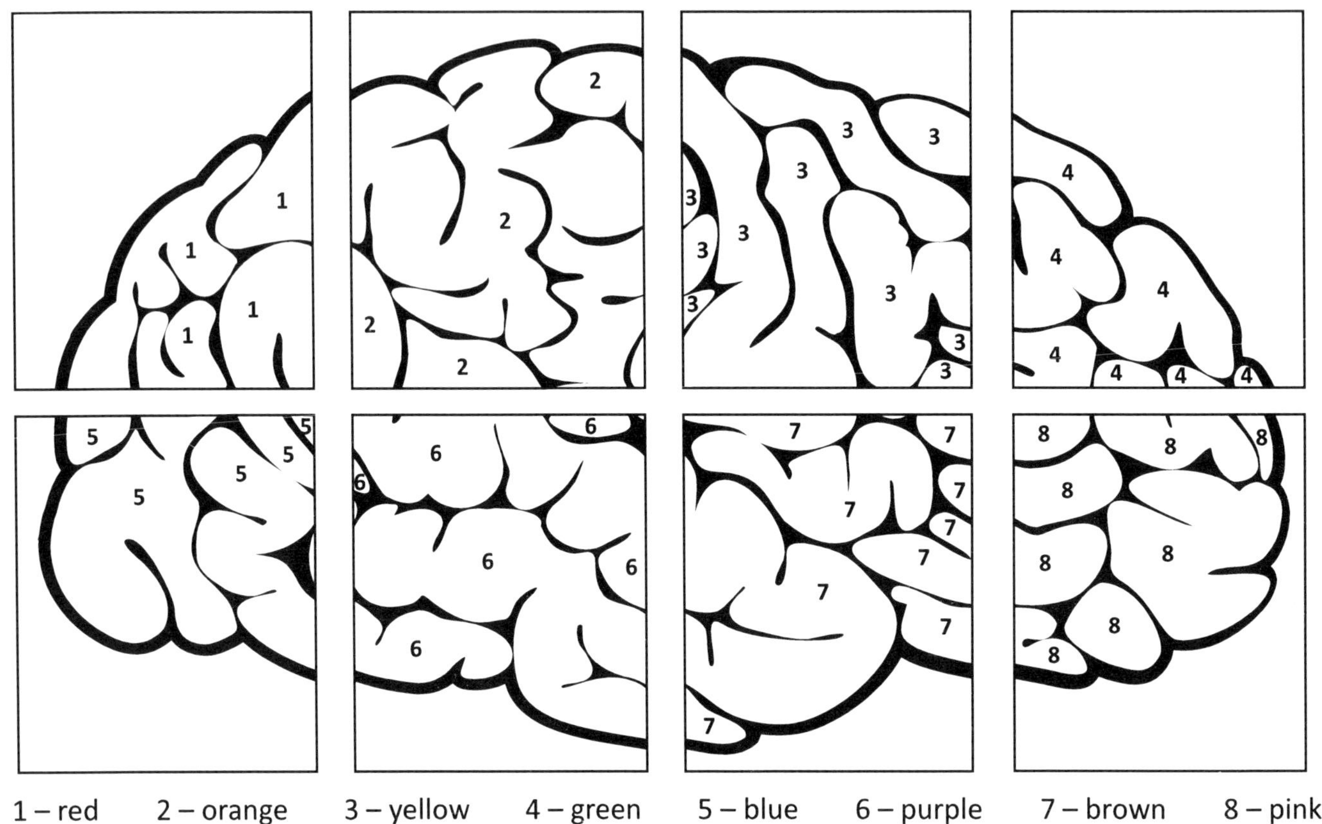

1 – red   2 – orange   3 – yellow   4 – green   5 – blue   6 – purple   7 – brown   8 – pink

Traced Verse

Directions: Trace the verse.

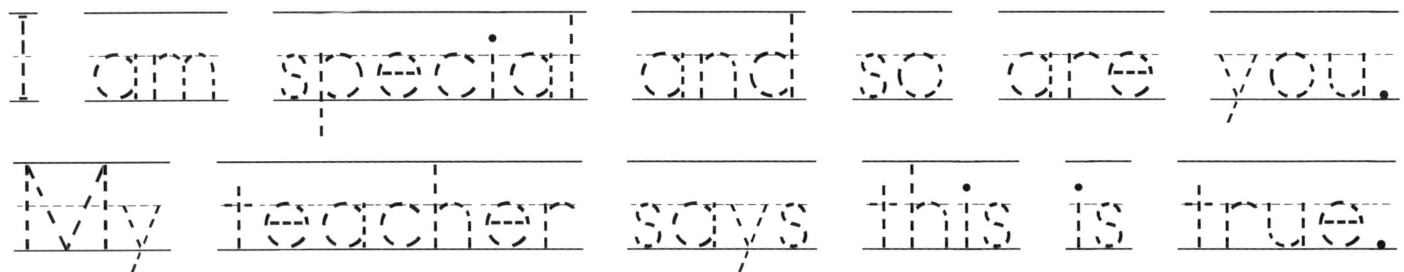

Handwriting Practice

Directions: Now copy the verse on the line below.

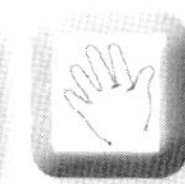

Directions: Cut out the picture boxes at the bottom of the page. Paste the pictures into the story where they belong. Read your story to a friend.

My Story

The  is a big place. There are lots of people. Each

 is special. It is good to  and take care

of people. It is good to  at people and to be kind.

This makes the world better.

Reproducible 3: Connect the Dots

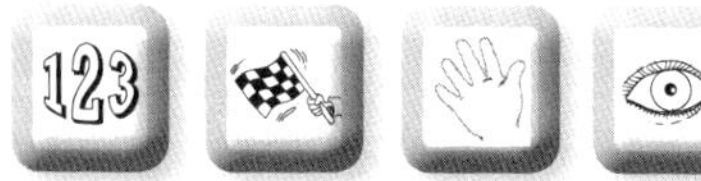

Directions: Place your pencil on the number 1 and connect the dots in order to 20. What picture did you make?

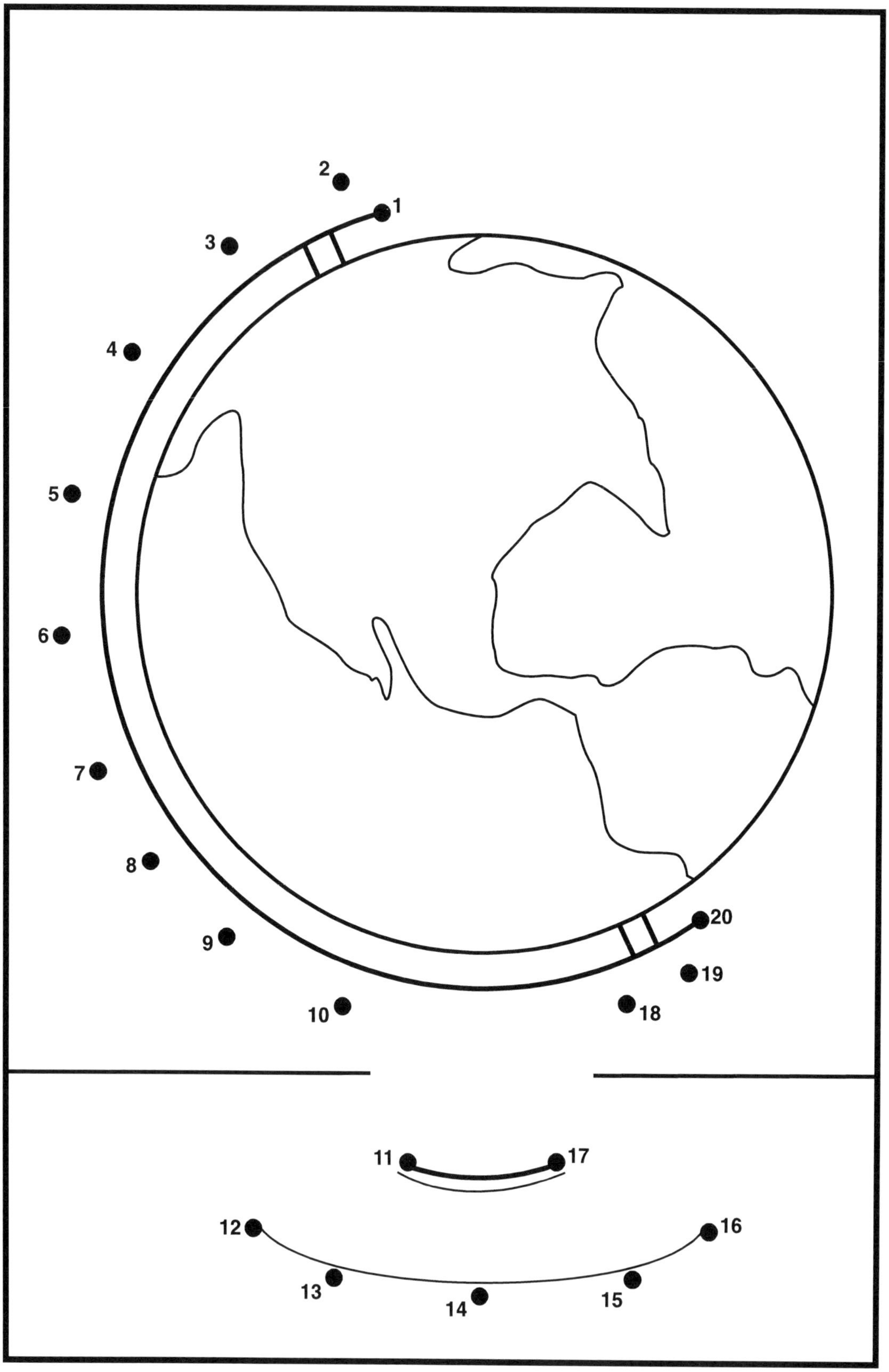

This is a picture of ____.

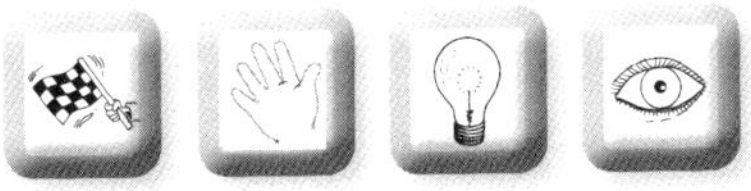

   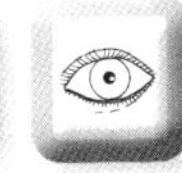

My name is: _______________________________ .

Directions: Put your pencil on the dot that says "begin," and find your way to the children who are playing together in the park.

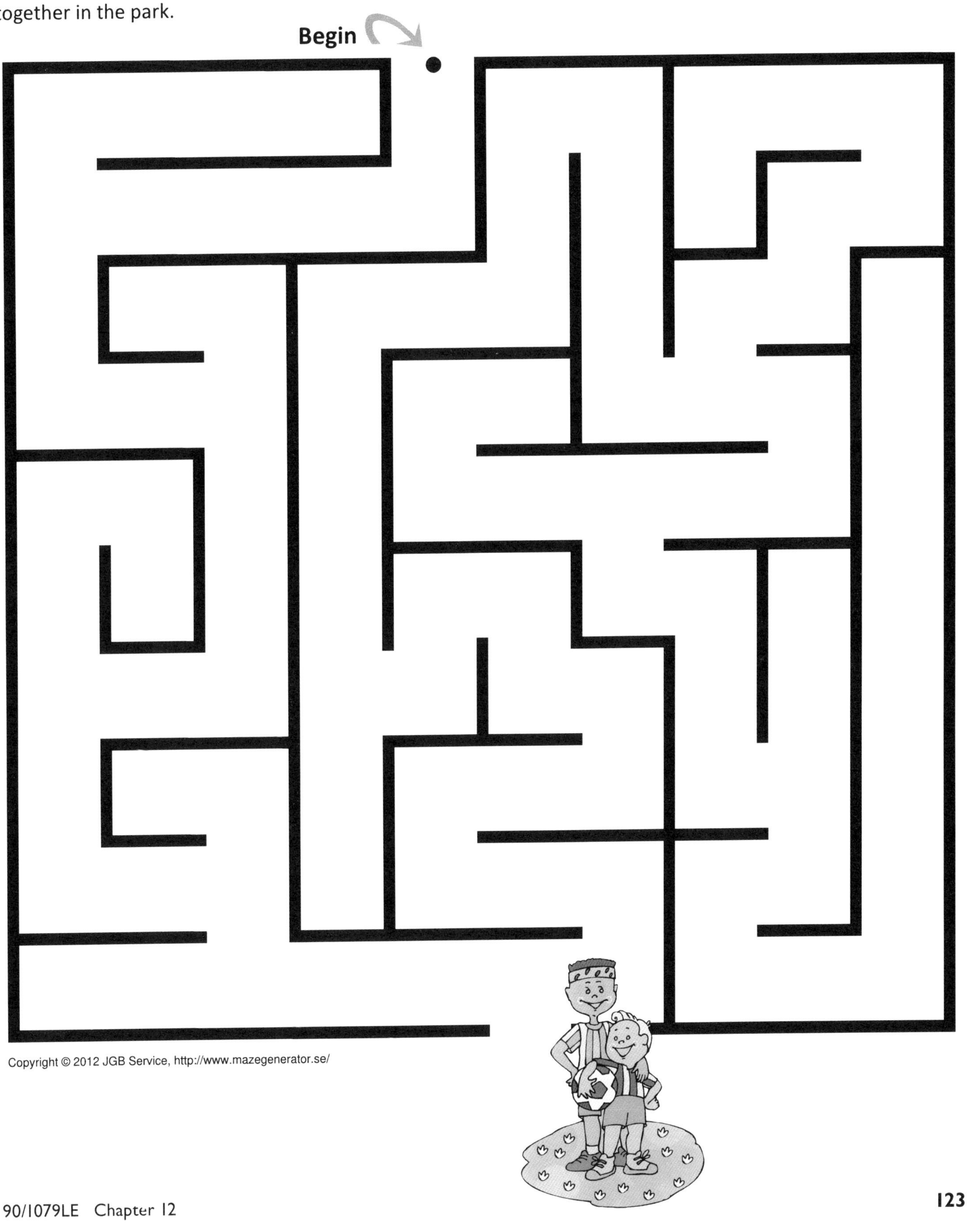

Begin

My name is: ___________________________________ .

Directions: Use cups of colorful puffed or circle cereal or math cubes to solve the problems as your teacher reads the prompts. Write the answer on the line. You may glue your solution into each box.

Juan has 5 puppies. Three of his friends adopt puppies from him. How many puppies are left at Juan's house? ___________________

Elena is helping her mother set the table for supper. She has 6 spoons for the soup. But there are 8 people in her family. How many more spoons does she need? ___________________

Chan and his friend Michael are going on a hike. They will be hungry. They will need 2 granola bars each. How many granola bars should go in the backpack? ___________________

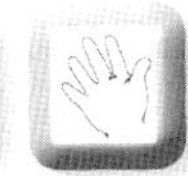

My name is: _______________________________ .

Directions: Draw pictures to complete each page of the booklet below.

<table>
<tr>
<td>

I am special.
I am a _______________ .

</td>
<td>

My favorite food is
____

</td>
</tr>
<tr>
<td>

I like to play with
____

</td>
<td>

My family is
_______________________ .

</td>
</tr>
</table>

 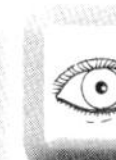  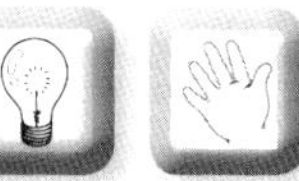

My name is: ______________________________________ .

Directions: Look at each row of pictures. One picture does not belong. Put an X on that picture.

1	  
2	  
3	  

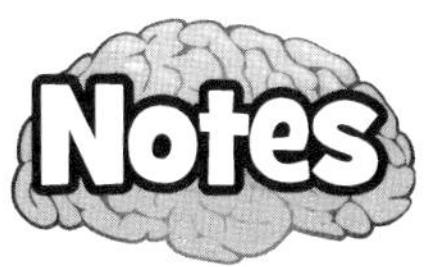
Notes

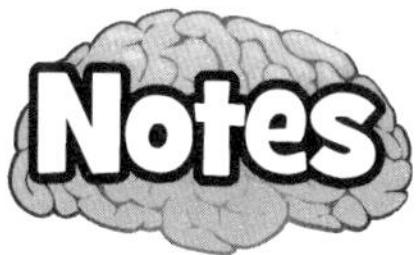